W9-BLC-792

Praise for
Handmade

"A rich life's worth of journeys both at the workbench and upon the trail, *Handmade* can show us the way out of the woods, sure, but even better, it teaches us that maybe in the woods is the place to be. Gary Rogowski leads us gently but surely upon the path to a type of success we may not have previously considered. (Hint: it involves blisters). The stories and lessons in this palatable tome portray the type of ignorance to which we should all aspire. Hats off."
—**Nick Offerman**, woodworker and author of *Paddle Your Own Canoe, Gumption,* and *Good Clean Fun*

"In *Handmade*, Rogowski writes of his love of tools, patience, discipline, the beauty and behavior of wood, learning to forgive his daily mistakes at the bench, why he believes in maintaining exceptionally high standards, and so much more of use to all who care deeply about craft and practice."
—*Foreword Reviews*

"Gary Rogowski has written an engaging biography that traces his development from a youthful student searching for a meaningful path in life to a highly respected and accomplished furniture maker and teacher. Alternating chapters describe his experiences as a woodworker and as a hiker and mountaineer in his native Pacific Northwest, illustrating his view that the lessons learned in each endeavor are the same. They are lessons in the quality of thinking that allows one to overcome internal barriers to internal goals. While furniture makers will recognize many of the lessons learned as their own, this book will appeal to anyone who has worked hard to identify and develop their own gifts."
—**Miguel Gómez-Ibáñez**, president, North Bennet Street School

"'Do good work. There will be evidence.' We would all do well to heed the advice of Gary Rogowski. He is one of those rare individuals who has come to peace with excellence. In this charming tale, he reveals a few of his secrets and plenty of his mistakes, so the rest of us might listen and learn. From tales 'of wood' to tales 'in the woods,' Rogowski's aim is true."
—**Joyce Cherry Cresswell**, author of *A Great Length of Time,* 2017 Oregon Book Awards winner in fiction

"Gary Rogowski loves to rock climb and also has a deep love for woodworking. Both disciplines require courage, concentration, and a developed sense of method; one wrong step, one wrong cut. Gary's book delves into this synchronicity with enjoyable anecdotes of climbing and woodworking interlaced with serious discussion of the importance of focus, practice, patience, and how we become masters of craft."
—**Roland Johnson**, contributing editor, *Fine Woodworking*, and author of *Taunton's Complete Illustrated Guide to Bandsaws*

"This is a book to inspire anyone who wants to do work that has meaning and purpose. It is also about becoming a creative, compassionate, and forgiving person through the pursuit of excellence in one's chosen vocation; the journey to craft mastery becomes a journey of self-realization. Gary reflects honestly and at times painfully on what his life and work have taught him and in so doing gives us permission to learn something about our own innermost feelings and aspirations. He is a role model for what education should be about: to provide us with the necessary creative and intellectual skills so we can become the person we know we can be."
—**Philip Koomen**, furniture designer and maker, Fellow of the Royal Society of Arts and the Chartered Society of Designers

"Reading **Handmade** is like sitting down with a friend full of stories and the hard-earned wisdom acquired in doing work he loves. Gary Rogowski is frank, affectionate, encouraging, unsparing, entertaining, and humble. He passes on to his reader a passion for making lasting things by hand, one creation at a time, a pursuit and skill little-honed and much-needed in our time."
—**Colleen Morton Busch**, author of *Fire Monks: Zen Mind Meets Wildfire*

"We need more books like this—more books about why-to instead of just how-to. Gary Rogowski does an excellent job of giving us a memoir of his own development as a craftsman, combined with a thoughtful exploration of the mindset that allows, or even compels, a person to have the discipline it takes to reach mastery step by step by step."
—**Jim Dillon**, woodworking instructor, Highland Woodworking, Atlanta

HANDMADE

Creative Focus in the Age of Distraction

Gary Rogowski

Linden Publishing
Fresno, California

Handmade
Copyright © 2017 by Gary Rogowski. All rights reserved.

All photos by the author, unless otherwise noted.
Cover photo ©2017 David L. Minick / Total Access
www.totalaccessphoto.com
Author photo by Justin Lambert, U.K.

Published by Linden Publishing
2006 South Mary Street, Fresno, California 93721
(559) 233-6633 / (800) 345-4447
WoodworkersLibrary.com

ISBN 978-1-61035-314-4

35798642

Printed in the United States of America
on acid-free paper.

Library of Congress Cataloging-in-Publication Data

Names: Rogowski, Gary, author.
Title: Handmade : creative focus in the age of distraction / Gary Rogowski.
Description: Fresno, California : Linden Publishing, [2017] | Includes index.
Identifiers: LCCN 2017054189 | ISBN 9781610353144 (pbk. : alk. paper)
Subjects: LCSH: Rogowski, Gary--Philosophy. | Woodworkers--United States--Biography. | Furniture making--Philosophy. | Creation (Literary, artistic, etc.) | Character.
Classification: LCC TT140.R64 A3 2017 | DDC 684.10092 [B] --dc23
LC record available at https://lccn.loc.gov/2017054189

Contents

Act One: Discovery and Surprise

Act Two: Practice

Act Three: Forgiveness and Mastery

Acknowledgments

To Dick Wheaton and Joel Aycock. The scientists, the friends who helped me skid off the highway and find a new path.

Jane Hester, I was nothing without your support.

Thanks as well to Bob Rashkin, Petros Panagopoulos, and Rich Coleman, my fellow travelers.

My gratitude to Merridawn Duckler for her belief in my work. To my writing buddies Joyce Creswell, Colleen Morton Busch, and to fellow authors Nick Offerman and Todd Oppenheimer, Anne Washburn and Gordon Dahlquist.

My thanks to Marc Hess, Miguel Gómez-Ibáñez, Rollie Johnson, Jim Dillon, Philip Koomen, Cameron Nagel, Jimmy Ruppa, the Writers Grind and Molly Dear, my friend. Thanks for all your help and support, for reading and for your listening all along the way.

My thanks to Harold Wood and Jim Piper who thought enough of my work those years ago to trade me for their fantastic photography.

Big shout out to David Minick for Handmade and the cover photo and his continued friendship these years.

Foreword

In the fall of 1989, I was newly married and sorely in need of a unifying piece of furniture. Having just moved to Portland, Oregon, I had no idea where to turn, so I asked a curator of a prominent local exhibit hall, who gave me three names, singling out one in particular for his unusual style. A week later Gary Rogowski was at our door.

My then-wife and I had decided that our most important piece of furniture should be a dining room table—hopefully a spacious one, constructed flexibly enough that it could hold forth when needed, but fold up to take a more supplementary position when not needed. With that in mind, we had found a photo of a classic, dark-wood, gate-leg table. You've probably seen the type—with hinged leaves that can fold down at the sides, partly covering the gathering of its legs.

Gary looked at the photo for a long moment, then shook his head. "I don't like this," he finally said. "It looks like a bug." After we all shared a laugh, a sense of uncertainty set in. Sure, the table doesn't look like much when in its folded position, but that's not its prime time; more important, this is how gate-leg tables are made. "Let me play with this for a few days," Gary said. "There has to be a better way to design a gate-leg table."

Before leaving, Gary said a few words about his preferred style, an eclectic mix he'd developed over the years that he called "Oriental Deco." We had little idea what he meant, but the work we saw in his portfolio was clearly expert and gorgeous, so we paid him to draw up some tentative designs and waited.

Some weeks later, Gary brought back a scheme for a large oval table that had a clean, somewhat modernist beauty when opened, and then an entirely different beauty when closed; in some ways, in fact, it was particularly stunning when folded up. The down leaves, which formed most of the oval on each side, swooped toward the floor and up again almost like a schooner. When the legs were folded up behind them, they formed a spare, geometric design that recalled the serenity of a traditional Japanese home.

The combination—a few strong lines rounded out by a gentle curve—did indeed have a Deco feel, with an Oriental spirit.

It has been nearly thirty years since Gary built this table—doing so, incidentally, only after mocking the whole thing up, several times, in cardboard, building it with stunning pieces of cherry wood, and hand-finishing it with round after round of elbow grease and his own proprietary series of wood oils. I have held onto this piece through a divorce, several moves, a remarriage, and the abuses of young children. To this day, anyone joining us for dinner remarks on the singularity of its design and the obvious quality of its workmanship.

During those thirty years, I have also come to know Gary as a friend, a fellow writer, and a deep thinker about what craftsmanship means in a rushed, computerized world where our daily experiences seem to get more superficial every day, with little understanding of the complex ingredients that real quality requires.

I have suspected that this book was coming for a long time. If the decades these ideas spent in gestation have been frustrating to the author, we the readers are the beneficiaries of his struggles. The result is a wild ride—part autobiography, part philosophical manifesto, part search for meaning in a time when eternal values are up for grabs. In the process, Gary takes us through the myriad, eclectic trails he explored to find his answers and achieve his own level of mastery. The terrain is endless, highly individualized, and of course partly uncharted. But that's what made it worthwhile.

Mastery, as you will soon discover, is not just a set of achievements, or even a level of skill. It's a state of mind: observant, unafraid, focused, patient. Once you have the keys to such an attitude, which Gary strives to hand you herein, you can use them to unlock any number of doors. That is a great blessing for those of us hoping to become master woodworkers, or masters of anything.

—Todd Oppenheimer
Editor and publisher of *Craftsmanship Quarterly*
www.craftsmanship.net

Preface

Dear Gary,

This note comes to you from the future. I am writing it years after you started to think about changing your life. It is of course one of the great mysteries and sureties of life that you can imagine the future, think you know its possibilities, and never be even close to getting it right.

I have penned this book for you and for others like you. For those who are considering a life of creating, these words will show how choices can resonate through a lifetime, that small things can influence in big ways, and that it is an intentional decision to build a life as an artist in this culture. It has consequence. It can be an act of forgiveness as well as one of creation.

Do good work.

Sincerely, Gary

Pre-amble

I am one of the loudest woodworkers there is. Don't think for a second that my forty-plus years at the bench building furniture has transformed my nature. I am given to swearing at myself and my mistakes loudly enough that God can hear me without his ear trumpet. I am persnickety to exasperation with myself, with my obsession for precision, and like some player in a Greek tragedy I am chained to this rock forever. I can be stunned into silence some days by the new problems I create for myself at the bench. I should know better and yet I act shocked by each new error, the most recent design flaw, a fantastic misplacement of tool or mortise.

It may surprise you then that my stumbling, erring ways allow me to produce any work at all. Yet somehow I have managed to make some very good things. I have worked at creating a life building furniture, which is a hard thing to do anywhere, and I have lasted at it.

Handmade furniture is not a need. It is a desire. Those of us who try to make a living at it are stubborn, focused, and ill-suited for polite office company and its politics. We love tools and wood and to solve problems. We love wearing many hats, taking on all sorts of roles throughout a job. Finally and most importantly, we love to talk to ourselves. We need to have this running dialogue, this duet of yin and yang, our left brain logic fighting our right brain shenanigans. It is a delicate balance between determination and caution based on our past failures. It is also important for us to be at the bench for that is where the voices quiet, where the healing begins. My story is not about building furniture. Building furniture is simply a metaphor. My story is about practice and forgiveness.

I do not claim to be the best woodworker in the world. I can design and build well and I can write. To put it more simply, I can walk and chew gum at the same time. One came naturally and the other took years of training. But I can walk and chew gum now at least. After some decades of building furniture, I penned two books on joinery and wrote for several magazines. Along the way, I started a School for Woodworkers, The Northwest Woodworking Studio, located in Portland, Oregon, a climate well-suited for work indoors at the bench. This is where I have taught and inspired folks about this craft.

Over this time I have also learned how to forgive myself my errors, how to fix most of my mistakes, and how not to point out the flaws in my work. I have learned when and how to pick up the pace. I have gained a fluency in my hands with my tools. I can make things look simple at the bench and amaze my students with the ease of my movements. I can perform a task in minutes that for them can take an hour. I am a master at woodworking. It is no contradiction. Just as a writer or composer struggles with his or her own demons in writing a story or song, one always brings one's quirks, one's habits, one's tics to the task of creating. The problem at the bench isn't the work, the challenges, or the mistakes—it is always me.

People assume that mastery of any type is a place that one reaches. It is a glow in the air that starts to become visible and hover around you. Or it is a corner that one turns on some fantastic day. These are pretty fantasies, pictures, show pieces, background images fit for a movie about a bygone era. Mastery, of anything, is an accumulation of experiences that, if you have a brain instead of rocks in your head, points out to you the truth of these things: you will get old, you can learn from your mistakes, and you should help others to their own truth. The things that you make will also accumulate and survive you.

Do your best with each job. There will be evidence.

If you work with your hands, I know who you are. If you have the desire to create and to make things, I am just like you. Let me tell you a story.

EDUCATION WORKS!

Few of us have any idea where our choices will put us. How the twists and turns in our lives will place us on paths we never imagined. I came to the West Coast in the 1970s to study literature at a small school called Reed

College. I had left the Midwest, where I had grown up in the fields outside of Chicago. Flat, steadfast, and certain: me and the fields. For my last two years of school I had transferred from a Midwestern university large enough to swallow a town inside its geography, the University of Illinois with its 30,000 students. I came to Reed with its 1,500 intellectuals. I came without visiting, without knowing anyone, without ever having been to the West Coast. I was bored with my life. I needed to remake myself away from my past, my friends, and my history. As if we can ever leave all these behind. They come with us of course in those tattered memory suitcases that we all carry around, the past, our traces, our lineage in time.

Reed was a small college, intellectually challenging yet oddly incestuous. I say of it, that I hated my two years there. I wish I had spent four. The students there stayed in this tempest, not venturing much into the city beyond, convinced of their intelligence and righteous in their arrogance. It was a place where one had to defend any idea, any statement, no matter one's state of sobriety. Priming myself there for a long life as a writer and teacher, I studied the great books. I tried and failed, as we all do, to grasp the idea of time slipping through my hands. Twenty-five years later, still living in Portland, I attended a reunion event at the college. I came upon an old professor of mine there.

> I tried and failed, as we all do, to grasp the idea of time slipping through my hands.

As a literature major I had enrolled in a class on the Victorians with the signature black sheep of the faculty at the time, Jim Webb. He was Badass, with a capital B, nicknamed "Spider God." He had the gaunt look of a smoker and drug addict made so popular by the Rolling Stones. Mostly dressed in black, always wearing colored sunglasses indoors, he presented an image not quite in keeping with standard academia decorum. If not hated by the administration, he was not popular with them for many things: his dress, his demeanor, certainly his attitude towards their authority and disdain for their methods of education. He was not popular for his stand on hiring a new college president. He had rented a billboard and plastered it with the face of the current college president asking: *Would You Buy a Used College From This Man?* In a campus of outliers, he was the furthest out.

For his class on the Victorians, we had started round a table in familiar Eliot Hall on campus, like most of my lit classes. We moved out to his house near campus to have our sessions soon after our first class. To convene elsewhere was a shocking enough concept then. A class not held in the confines of school? As if bricks could contain this man's ideas. The house itself stood as a nondescript small Tudor but inside the walls were painted black, the windows draped in black curtains. This made it seem that his class was more risky, more real, and we the students who had entered this world had it going on. "Yeah, man."

We studied the mystics such as Blake, Rosetti, and others like Ruskin. As in most literature classes at my college, discussions were replete with argument, logical discourse, and both ascendant and conquered positions. Our leader was by his nature very appealing to college age students: mysterious, intense, very smart, and just a little bit crazy, it seemed. One time in class debate I happened to cite the book we were reading as the proof of my cause. Making my point, whatever it might have been, I said, "It was there in the book." Jim Webb skewered me with this question: "You believe what you read in books?" My opponent in the debate chuckled at my naïveté. Ouch. It was no place for intellectual wimps. Defend your position.

Webb also wanted us, in our Victorian literature class, to get wood lathes, and to put these tools on his porch and start making wooden bowls and things just like Morris and Ruskin might have done. He lauded this approach of mingling literature and the crafts, melding mind and body. At the time, I scoffed at the thought. I imagined myself as a thinker, a writer, not a bowl turner.

When I saw him at that reunion, he sat on the ground under one of the giant beech trees near the commons where people congregated. It was a rare sunny day in June. He was sitting, legs crossed, spread out on a blanket, happy it seemed and wearing his characteristic enigmatic smile, his tinted glasses, and a cigarette. He was selling beads and things from his New Mexico hideaway where he raised goats and who knew what else, peyote probably, if you only asked for it. I saw him there and I immediately walked up to him. I introduced myself and said, "I took your Victorian literature class back in 1971 and when you said you wanted to put lathes on the porch so we could turn bowls I thought it was the most f—d up idea I had ever heard . . ." I paused. He was quiet. He looked up at me.

"I'm a woodworker now."

He jumped up into the air off his blanket and held up his arms and yelled, "Education works!"

Nice moment.

BELIEFS

It is my belief that working with our hands is valuable. Connecting with tools to create things offers us a compensation that no electronic calculus can bring. The cacophony that is the internet keeps us distracted, impatient, anonymous, and searching, but rarely satisfied. When we can see the results of our labor—paring with a chisel, using the needle and thread, creating with paint brush, soldering gun, or pen in hand—there is a different sense of accomplishment. It is a needed blessing in a hurried world to be able to say at the end of a long day, "I did this. Here are the results." It may only be an attempt to create something that feels solid in a world of impermanence, but this kind of progress means something to me in a day. Perhaps to you as well.

I have named this first section you've been reading the pre-amble. This is the stretch before we start our walk, which seems like a good way to begin a journey. It will give you a sense of what you're about to find here.

This is the story of a life given to a craft. I call it *memoirable* because it talks a bit about how I got here. It is also a discourse on the philosophy of Quality in a life. With the impetus provided by Robert Pirsig to the musings of Soetsu Yanagi, Twyla Tharp, Ted Kooser, and others, this book is a pronounced statement about the value of Quality in today's world. It is written to others as the century has turned and is headed faster than ever for uncharted territory.

I believe in the value of Quality, for the maker, the artist, and for the recipient. There is a resonance felt by all who come into contact with it. This idea swims into a cultural current that is strongly set against it, where Quality is currently more of a shape-shifter and less a beacon to steer by. The word is used now as a branding strategy, recalling an imagined better day gone by. Yet I believe that Quality has value in the life of the maker, for what he or she does to create, and for the recipients and users of this work. There is Quality in the making.

This is a book that trumpets the value of failure in an education, that posits that no one has life all figured out, particularly those who tell you that they do, and that if you aren't having fun by doing your work, you kill a part of yourself by doing so. Finally, as in most lives, the longer one hangs around, the more stories one can tell that can teach, make us laugh, and help illuminate ideas.

My own story is about stumbling onto the right path and staying on it. It is about the value of committing to an art and practicing skills every day until I got it in my bones. I simply propose that this can be your journey as well, even if you never touch a piece of wood but paint or sculpt clay or words instead. The struggle of the artist remains the same. You are not alone.

We are still humans, for all our digitizing of the world. Our needs, our desires, remain the same. We need to use our hands. We love to create. We can become very skilled. How we do this is both personal and universal.

When we build, let us think that we build forever.
—John Ruskin

ACT ONE:

DISCOVERY AND SURPRISE

1

The Smell of Sawdust

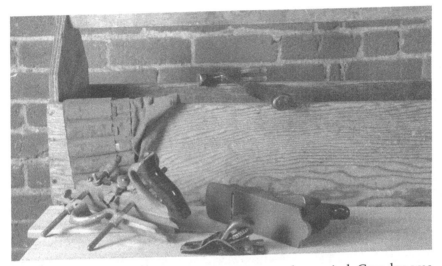

I was no woodworker as a youth. It never entered my mind. Grandpa was a carpenter, a coal miner, a bartender. We called him Dziadz. He lived with us for a time between jobs or wives. His first wife died, his second left him. I adored him because he always treated me with a mixture of great love and caution. Maybe he was afraid he would break me if he held me too hard with his iron grip. When I was small I remember him pointing out the western sun one dusk and telling me how it would move in the sky throughout the seasons. What other secrets did he know?

He could move anything with his pry bar, hammer, and shovel. He found work where he could, like any immigrant in the early twentieth century. He always worked with his hands. I couldn't help but see that one thumb of his was as wide as three of mine. He must have hit it with a hammer so many times that it just spread out in submission. Or maybe he nailed it just once really hard when he was drunk. Didn't he notice where he was putting it?

I remember him working at our farmhouse in Illinois for a time. He had built the saltbox-style house on farmland outside of Chicago, finding this small parcel on his way to go fishing at Lake Geneva. My family had moved from the city and taken it over from him when I was small. It was all country then, flat fields dotted with a few homes huddled together every few dozen acres so the tornados would have easier targets to blow down. There was always something for him to fix there, more carpentry needed for the house, or a chore for my dad.

As a young teenager I wasn't concerned with celestial movement but in keeping up with other kids. One day I was lifting weights behind the house on our concrete patio, trying to get as strong as my older brother. I was out in the sunshine grunting with an iron bar. Dziadz saw me and smiled. He walked past me over to where he had been working. He reached down to the ground and grabbed a 4x4 timber. He walked back to me, holding it by its end in one of his hands, and said, "Lift this."

Good guy. Polish sense of humor.

My father was a more-than-capable handyman. He knew tools and how to use them. He could mix and pour concrete, do electrical work. He transformed the old attached garage on our house into a living room. He made furniture for the new church, and built me a desk to study at. My brother and I did a list of chores for him around the house. We were also enlisted to carry his tools to fix the tractor, or to hold the light as he fixed the sump pump in the basement. He was always yelling at me for something. Or he would throw his tools down in disgust and scream at me for not paying attention to what he was doing. "Hold the ladder still, dummy."

It was easy to hate being around him working on things. If I complained, one of his favorite sayings to me as I grew older and could understand its significance was this bit of homespun warmth: "You know where you can find sympathy? Between shit and syphilis in the dictionary." As my friend Vinny used to say about people: he was a piece of work.

My dad, I realized later, was a three-year-old in the body of an abusive alcoholic. He could erupt over how someone passed the food. Spitting, sputtering, furious with the transgression. It's not how to act and yet this is what we learned to expect, the exploding father. He constantly proved that he could control the room with his anger. Maybe he learned it from his father, although I never saw that type of anger from Dziadz. Maybe he learned it in World War II or from the failures in his own life. It's no way to act—except maybe in battle—screaming your needs, your disappointments, your standards to the person across the table.

He of course had standards for me and my brother. His standards were simple and impossible to reach: nothing we did was ever good enough. Do it better. My mother couldn't stand up to him and my brother tried to follow his example of disdain toward me, just without the surprise explosions. Not surprisingly, I tended to shrink inside myself a bit. I developed an interior world to live within. I don't remember having any interest in how furniture was made. At that time I was more interested in throwing paper balls at the trash can than wondering how my father had built my desk. I sat at it doing homework, studying to avoid his belt, or worse, the verbal abuse. Punishment is quite an interesting mentor to a kid.

I have been asked by many people over the years, "Did you take shop class as a kid?" My response is yes. I didn't like it. I remember that my required talk in sixth-grade shop class, replete with visuals, was on wood screws. I do not remember being fascinated by my lecture. My mahogany bookends for class were nailed together and had the hasty grace of all my work then. It never occurred to me growing up that building furniture could be a choice in life. That being at the bench could be an act of forgiveness for me as much as a career choice.

Even through all this, one of my great remembered experiences of when I was little was being shooed out of our kitchen when the cabinetmaker came to build our new cabinets. He set up his sawhorses outside our house and cut up fir and plywood on them to make our cabinets, producing piles of sawdust and shavings that filled the air with the smells of his handiwork. I was entranced by the fragrance of the wood; somehow being around it made

> I could look at all the lumber and smell the wood. Sawdust smells like nothing else. I did not know until years later how hooked I was by this experience, how intoxicating this was to me at the time.

me feel good. What he was building made no difference to me. I loved the smell of that wood.

Going to the lumberyard with my dad was also a thrill because the warehouse was mysterious—who knew what happened here?—and cavernous. It was a cathedral to a small kid, with its tall, dim roof, only it was better than church because you didn't have to be quiet in there. Boards rose up into the dark insides of this timbered building. And there was that resiny aroma again wrapping its charm around me. I could walk around with my dad, which, even for all his yelling at me, always made me feel special when I was small.

I could look at all the lumber and smell the wood. Sawdust smells like nothing else. I did not know until years later how hooked I was by this experience, how intoxicating this was to me at the time. I forgot about it. I was a thinker, a dreamer, lost in my books and scribblings as I grew up. I wasn't going to work with my hands. I was going to get as far away from the world of my father as I could. Whatever he stood for, I would stand elsewhere. I was going to be a teacher of some kind. Maybe a priest or a scribe or a writer. And so I went to a college to study literature and the great books.

People ask, "How did you become a woodworker, then?" My reply was simple, "It was the scientists. They showed me the way."

> Things men have made with wakened hands
>   And put soft life into
> Are awake through years with transferred touch,
>   And go on glowing
> For long years.
> And for this reason, some old things are lovely
> Warm still with the life of forgotten men
> Who made them.
> —D. H. Lawrence

ABNER RIDGE

One of the scientists I knew at college was a physics major, Dick Wheaton. He was a motorcycle guy, a motorhead who loved fixing things, and an avid outdoorsman. He was a bit taller than me, just over six feet, and thin with large wire-rimmed glasses. He seemed imperturbable and was always happy facing a problem. His laugh ended on a high note even when laughing at himself. When I moved to the Pacific Northwest to finish up college, I started hiking and rock climbing in the Cascades with Wheaton. These mountains with their carpets of fir and hemlock have a flavor, a sense, a feeling about them that is suited for contemplation.

Hiking in the woods became wrapped up in my life as a woodworker. I never walked alone in these woods. There was always a throng of thoughts

marching alongside me in my head. Chattering away, these fragments and ideas, minor revelations and important discoveries, and thoughts about what a life should look like, all strolled with me as I took in the sights and sounds. Walking was a way of both clearing and filling my brain at one and the same time. I needed this movement to break ideas loose inside me, to stir things up, and to let thoughts settle.

Being on a trail, seeing the mist weaving fingers through the tall firs, watching these close clouds rise up off hillsides through the dark canyons, seeing the rocks and treetops—these sights drew me to pathways where I could let my mind wander. In Robert Macfarlane's lyrical book, *The Old Ways*, his story is about the concept of the path, the need we humans have for the journey. It is the walk itself, with its effort, its sacrifice, its tedium, or danger that is important because in the walking we get closer to the truths we hold inside ourselves. My own path to Mastery is one taken by many others before me, but like any path, my footsteps make their own mark upon it.

So too did these words of Thomas Clark, from his famous poem "In Praise of Walking," suit me:

In the course of a walk, we usually find out something about our companion, and this is true even when we travel alone.

When I spend a day talking I feel exhausted, when I spend it walking I am pleasantly tired.

> The pace of the walk will determine the number and variety of things to be encountered, from the broad outlines of a mountain range to a tit's nest among the lichen, and the quality of attention that will be brought to bear upon them.

～

Some things in nature have made a lasting impression on me. Rivers, waterfalls, mountains. One such location was a particular trail in the Cascade Mountains that I found with Wheaton: Abner Ridge, a place in the forest that seemed to call me back over time.

Wheaton and I, with my dog Joe Willie and two other hikers whose names are lost in memory, went for a hike up the Abner Ridge trail. We went up it one spring to scale the western face of the mountain as high as we could reach because someone had told us we could get pretty far up this way. We were young and energetic, with our new ice axes in hand, and we thought we could climb up the mountain anywhere. I do not remember the hike. Was it long or short? What did we see along the way? Had Wheaton's hands recovered enough from his accident to be trustworthy?

We drove into the Cascade Range on the west side of the mountain to a place called Daisy Plain. From there we walked in three or four miles to Klickitat Falls on a flat trail that was never straight but not hard walking. The falls were pretty enough that I wanted to stop and stare at them for a long time. There's a lot of worn ground there. Many feet have walked around these blue rivulets that tumble down a series of short rock falls, water rushing in a calm fountain of blue and noise, all hurrying down the rocks in the middle of the forest. It's glorious. But we had a hike to make, a mountain to climb, and needed to get moving. We'll see it again on the way back, I thought to myself.

From the falls we hiked four miles up a trail that was so long there were only three switchbacks in a two-thousand-foot elevation gain. It was unmarked on my USGS map but it started from the falls and headed up the long spine of Abner Ridge to the wilderness area. I put pencil marks on my map to indicate where we walked because on my map there was no trail marked out. Not this Abner Ridge trail.

I don't remember the walk being long or boring or inspiring. I remember only being up top at the tree line where trees cannot grow any higher up the mountain. It was cloudy out so there wasn't much to see. Occasionally the mountain would peek out at us from above. The trail had disappeared so we wandered around looking for a way up. We hadn't hit much snow yet, only a few patches. What we had run into finally were rocks. The humans could scale them with some effort, but not Joe Willie. We could push him up a few rock faces, but it was going to be tough getting him down. Even an able-bodied Brittany spaniel like him could not climb here. We tried one section and another. They were all too sheer for him to leap. So we said, that's enough.

I marked my map to record where we had been, going off-trail like we had. I thought I would be back soon. When I was young, I thought I'd get back to everywhere soon to retrace my steps. What could life possibly throw in the way?

So we gave up our ascent and tried glissading down some icy patches of snow using our ice axes as brakes. We ran along the snow and then jumped onto our backs to slide downhill and practice the arrest of our fall with our axes. Wheaton managed a decent arrest with his ax. With my first go at it, I stuck my landing and hit the icy snow so hard I felt like I had broken a rib. Maybe I did. I could barely breathe without pain so I stopped my ax practice right there. It was one of several accidents that seemed to walk with us on this hike. We returned, me gasping for breath the whole way home. There my memory of the hike stops.

And on my map still are those pencil lines indicating where I thought we had gotten to. On the map, right at its edge, before it disappears into the whiteness of where the next map would begin, it says, *View.*

2

The Scientists

My first year at college in Portland, I found a house to share with four others in the northeast section of town miles from campus. One housemate, Bill, was a physics/literature major, wrestling with two dissimilar worlds. He had physicist classmates over one afternoon to drink beer. I saw immediately that they thought about the world in an unusual way. My own knowledge of physics began and ended with my deep understanding that the sun is in the sky and it is made up of atoms that are hot. What else did I need to know?

I was fascinated by how these scientists could talk for hours about the universe as a giant whirling mass of gases and then have a different discussion about atoms smashing into each other or galaxies expanding or collapsing. They seemed to talk like they had some knowledge of how the world actually worked. They knew about gravity and astronomy, particle physics, like Bobush, the Russian theoretician ("death to the Bolsheviks"), and Petros, the suave Greek lover. They knew about solar systems, galactic black holes, and motorcycles, like Joel the astronomer and Wheaton the motorhead. Or how to fix a motorbike that I had dumped. I'm still sorry, Joel. And if they really did not know, then they sure talked a good game, with real joy and interest in the subject. I was very curious about how they approached things. Their chatter was so different from my own. It had nothing whatsoever to do with foreshadowing or imagery or metaphor. Of all the disciplines practiced in my halls of learning, the people with whom I felt the most affinity walked in the halls of the physics labs.

One night four or five of us had gone out to Pine Mountain to view the moonrise. This was a small mountaintop about an hour outside of town up a river gorge. The physicists knew the full moon was upon us that clear night, so we headed out to drink some beer and smoke and discuss important things. We walked out to a promontory, climbed over the outlook's fence and onto the rocks staring east toward the mountain and the moonrise. In the course of that night, as we started to shiver, the active brains of the physicists took over in a feat of phenomenal mental calisthenics.

One of them asked if it was possible for pee to freeze before it hit the ground. More importantly, could it pull the perpetrating pisser over? Hilarious and stupid all at once, but the argument went on about temperature and molecules and ammonia content in all seriousness for them. I jotted this night down in my memory as I stared at the full moon wondering about these guys. These were not small questions for them. This was physics! I was fascinated. Physicists were always asking, "What would happen if I did this?" But the weather was not severe enough to test anyone's theory, so there was no agreed-upon conclusion.

I realized then that there was another way of being in the world. I was an intellectual of sorts when I graduated, halfway pregnant with possibility—my wry adage—and I thought I could do almost anything well. But really my years of schooling had left me prepared to write pages on almost any literary subject without saying anything much of value. I was ready to accept a Pulitzer Prize for my novel, yet to be written. In truth I was lost. I was done with schooling but had nothing to take its place. All I had known was reading, discourse, ennui. I bummed around Portland that summer, picking up odd jobs and drinking quarts of beer in the park with other bums like myself, trying to find something that sparked me. Anything to spark me.

I read some books that started to push me about what a personal philosophy might look like. What kind of world could I create for myself? I read John Muir's amusing and folksy treatise on mechanics, *How to Keep Your Volkswagen Alive: A Manual of Step-by-Step Procedures for the Compleat Idiot*. I also picked up the seminal book for my time, *Zen and the Art of Motorcycle Maintenance*, by Robert Pirsig. I began to think that maybe one could be a philosopher and still wear overalls. Do real work, get your hands dirty, and yet still be thoughtful. This was a completely different world view where physical labor was not demeaning, where one could think about stuff like cause and effect while working with your hands. Where one didn't have to look like an intellectual and have initials behind your name in order to be one.

I had listened to my scientists discuss their cryptic ideas. I poured these closely watched things into my own beaker of philosophy that I carried around with me, the one filled with ideas about beauty and art and nonconformity. I snapped then to a kind of attention about my own life. Mine had been mapped out by my own sense of fear, by my own former impulse to conform, to do the right thing and make the right choice in an attempt to please the authority figures in my life. I knew now that this was an impossibility since my father was rarely happy with my results; same with that religion I had once so keenly adhered to. No pleasing that god. We were already born stained. How can I be guilty before I did anything? While perfectionism might be ingrained in me, I could turn it onto a new path and try something completely out of the mainstream that I had been raised to wade into.

I moved into a drafty two-story-tall house that was tucked back into some trees out of sight of the neighbors. There was a rutted, potholed road to it grandly called a drive, and another gravel road called a court I drove on through a stand of trees, disappearing into the woods. Across from the house there was a spot that had been carved out into the blackberry patch, our garden, our retreat into nature. I went out there one night to sleep under the summer stars and a barefaced possum and I scared the crap out of each other when we both walked into that patch together. The place had a nice feel to it, and the house was a grand place to be driftless. Room outside to sleep in your sleeping bag or tuck in on a couch. There was a large old clawfoot tub in the bathroom to bathe in. The band—of course there was a band—practiced downstairs and we lived in this dilapidation, surrounded by nature and hidden from prying eyes so that one could think grand thoughts undisturbed. Perfect.

One day exploring around the side of the house, I found two things that intrigued me. One was an old wooden hand plane and the other a piece of wood. The plane had metal fittings and a blade fixed into a long, wood body. I didn't know it at the time but it turned out to be a transition-style jack plane. The wood was cracked and the fittings were rusted. It said something to me, murmuring a potential of some sort. This was the kind of tool I saw in the hands of the cabinetmaker when I was young. The other thing I found nearby was a half-round chunk of wood that had fallen off the outside of a log some time ago. Its bark was off and its outer surface was smooth while the inside was scooped out like the round of the tree it had once been a part of. The whole piece was maybe three feet long and shaped like the seat of a bench.

Here was a tool and some wood. Had someone out here tried to use them, one on the other? Or had they thrown them away in disgust? Who knew why I found them in the ferns and blackberry vines? Somebody could do something with these things, if only they knew what they were doing. Not me, but somebody could. These two objects hinted at something, about another way of living perhaps. What they ended up doing for me was magic. I just didn't know it at the time.

> If a piece of steel or a piece of salt, consisting of atoms one next to the other, can have such interesting properties: if water—which is nothing but these little blobs, mile upon mile of the same thing over the earth—can form waves and foam, and make rushing noises and strange patterns as it runs over cement; if all of this, all the life of a stream of water, can be nothing but a pile of atoms, how much more is possible?
> —Richard P. Feynman, *Six Easy Pieces*

Snow Camping

Wheaton and I had become very interested in snow camping and how to survive in the wilderness. Part of the appeal was getting all the equipment together: the sleeping bag, parkas, gloves, the gaiters for your boots, the Snow Lion tent for camping outdoors in any kind of extreme weather, the snow booties for keeping your toes warm at the campsite. The list, the gear, the preparation was as much a part of the appeal as the ordeal itself. And I think for Wheaton it was also a test of his abilities. What could he do with his hands now? How far could he push himself? His accident with his hands had left him damaged but he was determined.

That winter my brother had invited us to join him and his pal in the Mount Roosevelt wilderness area to try our hand at cross-country skiing. They had skied a time or two before so they were much quicker than us on skis. Wheaton and I had on our rented wooden skis and were just learning to kick glide along. Forget about trying to figure out the right wax to use in the wet, then frozen, Oregon conditions. It was enough to be able to stand at first with a pack on. Then we had to unstick our skis from the wet snow we had been sinking into and get moving. These were heavy skis so we didn't get up much speed, even on the flat section of terrain that we were on. At first it was every fifth glide that produced a frantic waving of the arms and poles and then a prodigious flop into the snow. Eventually we got the hang of it but it took the most part of a morning. My brother abandoned us after a few hours in his enthusiasm to ski off on a longer trail. We didn't see him again on that trip. It was okay to be moving at our pace so we let him go on as it had started to snow some flakes. There was no way we could keep up with him anyway, being such new ducklings on the snow.

We skied back some distance to the car to get our camping gear and then skied back to an open site where we pitched our tent in the light falling snow. I could never figure out the knots that Wheaton's fingers managed to tie so quickly into the tent lines. He used some kind of a self-arresting knot he could snug up when the lines got slack from the wind. His fingers flew in his knot-making as if they didn't want to be seen. We climbed into our sleeping bags and played some cards, enjoying our relative comfort. At nightfall we made some dinner, smoked some cigarettes because we both had that foul habit then, and drank some cheap whiskey outside by the heat of a camp stove. Then we settled in to sleep.

It snowed all night. We didn't hear it out there in the woods of course. It was still and quiet and peaceful all night. The tent door was surprisingly hard to open the morning. It was stiff in fact. Two feet of new snow greeted us that dawn. We pushed the door out and crawled out into the light to see that the tent was half covered up with snow. It was the kind of surprise that lit me up with joy and then made me look hard around myself. A new snowfall in the forest is gorgeous and brilliant and beautiful, smothering everything with a white sheen of freshness. The tree limbs bend under its weight, loaded with snow on their tops like too much icing on pieces of cake. The ground is no longer marked. It is hidden, soft. The trails are gone. Footprints are covered. Skis are buried and turn into small white trees.

The snow laid a coverlet of beauty and reflected light on everything. It also covered up tracks. It was quiet and so dangerous if we made a mistake. Out in the snow, warmth is critical to survival. We had to stay warm so we went back into the tent to consider our options. We had food, water, and a warm place to sleep. We were fine. Why worry for now? Besides, our car was buried in the snow too.

Wheaton and I decided to wait it out to see what was coming. We got back into our sleeping bags and stayed toasty playing cards, peeking out the door every once in a while to check on the weather. After a few hours, a light wave of snowflakes started to fall on us. We considered that another snowfall might bury us for good. Our trail in was already covered so we knew we had to kick out in fresh wet snow anyway. We had to get out. One of us had to find a route through the trees and kick a path through the snow while the other would follow carrying extra weight in their pack as the trade-off. It would be a labor getting back and finding the car. We had plenty of light for now so we loaded up our gear and got to work finding our way back through the whiteness.

It still amazes how tracks in the snow can leave such an impression on the mind. That was the only time I was on that cross-country trail with Wheaton. I remember it better than yesterday. How calm he was and ready to act when the time came. There was no panic, just consideration, and then movement when the time was right.

3

Jake the Mechanic

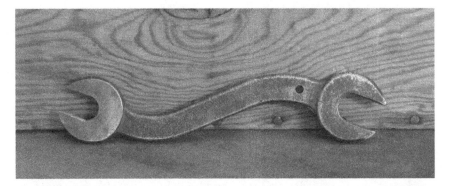

I needed to leave town for a time to figure out my direction in life. It was one of my roommates, Claudia or Billy, that I left that hand plane and wood with. I drove back to the Midwest and made it as far as Ann Arbor, Michigan, to stay with a friend. It was where I got a job as a car mechanic. Check that, as a VW mechanic. Because of Muir's *Idiot* book, I figured out some simple things that I could do on a VW and lied my way into this job. My own VW convertible was going to need an engine rebuild soon so I worked hard and I worked cheap and they kept me on. I had the worst bay in the garage to work in through a winter. The one by the floor drain. This meant that all the snow from the other cars around me would melt into my slot, so I worked in a puddle of water most of the time. Not ideal conditions in the cold of winter there, but, hey, I had a real job working with my hands, so this was exciting and different.

As it turned out, I was no gearhead. Too many blood sacrifices to the wrench gods were required. This was the sort of career move that proved that I needed to consider my future better. I wasn't quick, so my boss was providing welfare to this long-haired hippie who could work hard and was trying to do his best for his $100 a week.

In Michigan working on cars, rust always won the battle. I was constantly being stumped by its iron grip on parts. We would get these VW Bugs into the shop and the muffler that needed replacing would be rusted on tight or the heat exchangers were rusted shut. My job was to hammer away on these buckets with my air chisel, trying to get their nuts and bolts to budge while lying on my cart underneath them, and usually getting nowhere.

Now an air chisel is a pneumatic tool powered by compressed air and is so noisy that the only way you can work with one is right up close to it, immersed in its syncopated racket. The noise from an air chisel is manageable because you feel like you're getting something important done. On the other hand, your neighbor using one for an hour is a cretin with no imagination. "Get leverage!" is what I wanted to scream at him. He also has no brain left after all the ruckus he has created. His air chisel is a shriek, a crime against your eardrums, a cacophony of havoc, and this perpetrating neighbor should be caged or chained up or incapacitated somehow. Someone of a sensitive nature might think this.

It was an affront to your senses, this tool. We had to use it to free up parts because nothing else would work. We all did so with no earplugs, working in these tin box Volkswagens that resonated like marching band bass drums. I would crawl inside or under a Bug and hammer away at some stuck part, my mind tense, my arms and body jumping with the pounding of the air chisel. And it was fun at first making noise. But every once in a while I would come across some rusted-up section I could not free, even as I grimaced and pounded and hammered.

My best friend and savior when things went awry for me there at the shop was Jake. He was the kind of mechanic who didn't say much. Not much taller than me, he had a lanky calmness to him with a simple face and straight black hair parted so it fell flat across his head. It seemed to match his demeanor. He liked to size things up before he spoke. When I would finally recognize defeat, I would walk over to ask Jake for his help. Jake was maybe fifteen years older than me and very measured in everything he did. To my way of thinking he was the best mechanic in the shop, even if he wasn't the one rebuilding motors. To me he was the best because whenever I got stumped he could always figure a way out.

I would sidle across the aisle to Jake's bay and patiently wait for him to come up from underneath a car or from inside its hood. I had to ask him again for help, which he always generously gave. We were on a clock for each job so this was an imposition, make no mistake about it. I would explain the problem to him, which he understood immediately. In short, the issue was that I was a knucklehead.

Jake would stop what he was doing, climb out of the Volkswagen he was working on, wipe his greasy hands on a red rag, and come over to help me. I'd show him the rusted problem and Jake would take my air chisel and put its tip on the offending bolt and just stare at it. Then he'd move the chisel to the other side of the bolt and stare at that view for a while, just looking at things. Sizing things up.

No noise.

No action. Just looking.

And he would do this for a time, with me wondering why he wasn't making noise with that air chisel. But I was patient for he was bailing me out again. He'd pick his spot and blast away at it until the part broke loose. He was a genius in my mind. Calm, never in a hurry, and always successful. He would plan his leverage, the mayhem of the air chisel, and then perform the surgery in such a measured and violent way that it always succeeded. It wasn't just rusty nuts and bolts that Jake could master. It seemed that once he put his mind to it, he could always figure out a way to solve any mechanical problem. It was the sort of brainpower I stood back from in awe. He would stare at the problem until he knew where to put the lever, how to loosen the pin, where to take up the slack. Then, and only then, would he apply the force. No useless motion, no wasted moves, no loss of energy. Jake was a master in mechanics and no one gave him much credit for his intuition, his generosity, or his knowledge. I think mostly because he was no self-promoter. He never pointed at himself proclaiming his greatness. He went about his work quietly, with honesty, and a need to do each job well.

∽

I learned a lot watching Jake work. I learned about patience and planning, although I admit it took many years for these concepts to sink in for me at the bench. I learned that it's better not to thunder against a problem. Look at it critically and then unravel it. Did I mention that it took many years for this to sink in? It is difficult at first, no question.

At the bench some years later my patience came slowly to me. I made the cut; I checked the fit. A little more wood needs to come off. This work needs concentration and a great patience. I describe joinery, the art of putting pieces of wood together without nails or screws, as an act of accuracy plus patience. Eventually I developed that needed quality. I learned how to sneak up on a fit. I learned how slowing down made things go faster.

I had to stop like Jake to size up the problem. The problem is not going anywhere. Take some time. Be patient. Learn when to slow down, and then when I decide how to solve it be forceful and on the mark.

✍

I got a piece of advice from Jake one night at dinner over at his house with him and his wife. After the meal he told me, "Get out of this work. You're no mechanic. You're not right for it. You should be doing something else with your brain. Do something that will challenge you." He was right. I knew it. I was killing a winter there. When I got my own VW fixed and running right I drove back to Portland.

LOST AT THE BENCH

Hiking and time spent on the trail considering things were important. That space and quiet gave me the chance to mull over questions about my future and what I wanted to be. It turned out that being at the bench itself was another kind of pathway. There is plenty of opportunity during the building of a piece for musing about the future and the past. This is one of woodworking's allures. Once I can turn my hands loose on a task, I am free to go back in time or imagine what I could do or maybe start to design that next piece a little. But it is also true that this train of thought, my concentration, a whole job, can stall for lack of the smallest item required for the journey. It can come to a dead halt for the want of a single tool.

✍

An accumulation of tools of course is standard. Once I realized that this was the work for me, then I also realized how many tools are required for any job. This is the first hook, of course, for any woodworker—the tools. When I started to gather enough, I could walk to my bench and look at them all, this Miracle of Tools there on my wall.

There are the important measuring and marking tools. The tape measure is for long measuring and the 6" rule, my standard for measuring, is for very precise work and goes in my apron pocket. Then there are my squares, my straight edges, my diagonal rods, and my winding sticks. Cutting tools seemingly have no end in sight in my cabinet. I have saws for rough work and saws for cutting joints, carpentry saws, coping saws, fret saws, back-saws for precise work, both European push and Japanese pull saws. As for chisels, I now have only three sets that I use, but a fourth waits in the wings. Chisels for paring, ones for hard chopping, chisels for carving, and ones for delicate shaping. Hand planes, although much larger, proliferated like fruit flies once I started to collect them. My planes from my dad are there but have been supplanted by the best hand plane in my shop, my Lie-Nielsen low-angle block plane. There are smoothers and jack planes, a #3, a glorious #5¼, and my long and heavy #7, which once in motion requires a calculation for stopping distance. Rasps and files, scrapers and spokeshaves are all hanging close by. The list goes on.

Besides this Miracle of Tools, at the bench hung another incentive: the number of hats that I got to wear throughout a single build. There are so many jobs that a furniture maker must take on in the successful completion of a project. First there is a design to be properly stolen, from good sources of course. All design is a mash-up of others' ideas, but choose good models and steal boldly. Combine a number of good ideas together to make this new design particularly your own. That's first; a design has to be had.

> Besides this Miracle of Tools, at the bench hung another incentive: the number of hats that I got to wear throughout a single build.

Next, I needed wood. So I had to go choose the lumber, the right materials, the prettiest boards, flat and not twisted, without knots or with interesting ones. Then I needed to get it home to my shop safely somehow. I used my VW convertible, with the passenger seat removed and the top down, as my hauler for years.

Okay, I had the wood. Now I had to mill it into chunks, the right chunks. Don't waste any. It's precious stuff. Where do I cut? How do I saw it to bring out the beauty of this wood? What happens if the wood moves as I cut it? I'm a sawyer now. This is an important job as it's another form of design. It's just done with a saw and not a pencil.

Joinery is next. Which joints do I use and can I cut them? Do I have the knowledge, the tools, the patience? These are important decisions because they impact the design, if I'll make any money on the piece, and how long it will last. Then once the piece is assembled, I have to shape and sand it, add the magical details that will make it stand out in a crowd, and put a glorious finish on it so people will want to touch it.

All these tasks lie ahead of me. Yet I will get to none of them, they will all wait their turn, time will stop, if I can't find my 6" rule.

～

I couldn't find mine one day. Now I had lost things in the shop before. Some are lost forever, swallowed up in a pile of sawdust and then swept up. Maybe they were stolen outright by the gremlins for their own heinous purposes. It's hard to know. I have searched for hours for things that were right on my bench. I have also found it important to look for a lost item immediately, while the trail is still warm. If I let even an hour go by, the piece will get farther and farther away and be a lost orphan out in the world somewhere.

One day I put my 6" rule in the back pocket of my pants, instead of in my shop apron where it lives, because I was busy, I was distracted, and the job was a bit late perhaps and I needed to move on and do the work and just get it done and make this cut, which I had to measure, and I did and I often do this, you know, walk from one side of the shop to the other, and then I set down my ear muffs on the bench, and then I walk back to the saw, and where are my ear muffs? I ask, and they're across the room on my bench so I have to go back there and get them and start all over again and make this cut and . . . I . . . stopped . . . dead.

Where is my 6" rule?

It should be in my apron.

I looked. It wasn't there.

I went to the table saw. No sign of it camouflaged on its gray cast-iron surface. I walked back to my bench. Nothing. I checked my apron again. Empty of my rule. I looked on the floor under my bench. I checked what I thought was my last circuitous path. Maybe I had laid it somewhere. I checked the other benches, the band saw. Not there. I spent the next half an hour in search of a 6" piece of metal, going from bench to cabinet to machine and back again and I could not find it. This is one of the most important measuring tools of my life at the bench. I needed to find it. I tapped my breast pocket, not there. I looked in my apron again. I implored the tool gods, "This time I'll be good, this time I won't swear at you, just please give me back my 6" rule." I wanted to weep in frustration. I wasted time searching. I swore out loud anyway, I cursed my stupidity, I searched my bench again. I walked and looked under the saw, on the floor. "Where could it be," I wondered aloud. And the cycle began again in eagerness, because I remembered being in a spot where I had once had it, then to sadness when the tool was not found there, over to despair that it was lost forever, moving on to entreaties to the gods, and to the tool thieves. I have left chocolate out for these damnable elves and then walked away in the hope that they would have pity on me. "Give me back my tool," I cried out to them that day in anguish. And this pout, this fervent cry, made my nose runny. So I grabbed for my handkerchief in my back pocket.

Sigh.

4

Something Useless and Beautiful

Photo by Harold Wood

I was back in Portland trying to find work when one day in a parking lot I saw a guy wearing a madras bucket hat. He stood next to an old Ford pickup with a wheelbarrow on his rack and looked like a pleasant sort. I walked up to him and asked him if he needed help. Harvey poured concrete. He said he'd give me a try. Harvey was a good guy, very low-key, and I made it at the job longer than most. The job itself, called flat work, turned out to be an interesting choice: sidewalks, driveways, the occasional basement or foundation for a house. It was backbreaking, knee-destroying work. I could handle it okay because I liked working hard and I was outside where I could dream about where I was headed.

Harvey was a man of many talents it turned out. He also built furniture. He would pick up the Sears catalogue and find a piece in it he liked and he'd say, "I'm gonna build that." He would go out to his overflowing garage and make some room around that table saw of his, and he would build himself a piece. I thought to myself, Hmm, if Harvey can do this . . .

Later I saw a small exhibition of some handmade furniture at my former college where a professor, a scientist of course, had helped arrange the showing of some work of a former student. I started thinking, Why not? Why not do something completely different? It had a curious kind of appealing illogic to it.

My friend Joel, the motorcyclist, astronomer, and trail kicker for the forest service now, had decided to buy a metal lathe, which he put in the garage in front of his tiny three-room house. Since he was working metal in his free time, I thought I would work with wood. It smelled better. He let me set up a space there in this one-car palace.

My ideas of how things got made were still unformed. I thought everything was built at one factory: the telephone wires, hardware, and the poles that held them were all extruded out of the same plant somewhere. Things just appeared out of a Charlie Chaplin–like assembly line or by some gargantua of a machine that made the pole, the wire, and the insulators and the metal ladder steps stuck into their bottom, all ready to go into the ground. What did I know about making things? Tools? What could I do with tools?

First thing I built was a bench attached to the inside wall of Joel's garage. To test it I got up on it with my work boots on and jumped up and down (a particular test for strength no longer in use).

It amazed me to think that I could build with my hands like this. I remember walking out to the garage one day and pulling open the garage door and thinking to myself with a smile, Who knew? Look at what I'm doing. Who knew that this was possible? That I could do this? I was so astonished that this change had occurred, looking back a few months from where I had started. I was as pleased by its surprise as by the actual work.

On the other hand, I thought as I worked, my grandpa was a carpenter, and my dad had built furniture once upon a time. It was in my blood, wasn't it? It made sense. The work stretched my mind in ways it had never been stretched before. It was both mentally and physically challenging. I had to learn about tools and relearn geometry and figure out how to construct things so they wouldn't collapse of their own weight. It was exciting. It felt good to be so ignorant. There was a whole world of learning to discover. I came from a place so opposite to this one of cause and effect. I was from a world of argument, logic, and discourse that was so different from this world of design and geometry and danger that I could come to this new one with a fresh perspective.

At the same time, my approach to building furniture was always from the vantage point of beauty. For if I learned anything as a lit major, I thought that I had learned how to appreciate beauty and simplicity and structure. I learned to ask the question, Is this beautiful? My choice to teach myself furniture making was infused by my desire to create things. I didn't even know what kinds of things then. I wanted to create things of beauty. Even with no clearly defined standards of design at the time I knew I had to make great objects. I wanted to be doing this learning on my own too. Why not me? Why couldn't I do something useless and beautiful?

It is a strange courage
You give me:
Shine alone in the sunrise
Toward which you lend no part!
—William Carlos Williams, *El Hombre*

PINE MOUNTAIN TRAIL

My hiking boots were the steel-toed ones I wore when I worked pouring concrete with Harvey. They made for a decent hammer when a board needed to be moved just a bit. They also added on a bit of extra weight for hiking, as you can imagine. I didn't care. I was young, impossible to hold back, impatient. I couldn't wait to get up mountains with all the energy I had. So when Wheaton, in more appropriate footwear, and I and Joe Willie set out to climb up Pine Mountain, starting at the bottom, at river level, I was ready to go.

The trail starts at Multnomah Falls out in the Columbia River Gorge. The falls are a glorious, spectacular, long cascade of water and one of the longest drops of water in North America. Folks line up to see it. We parked the car and strolled past the old stone hut serving as lunch outlet plus latrine stop. We walked up the concrete pathways to the viewing bridge. There we had to stop to watch at least one bucketload of water come racing off the top of the falls and separate into cups and then a plume and then droplets to plummet down by gravity's decree into the pool of thundering water and then turn to mist and rise up again.

We hiked on up the trail to where we could be at the top of the falls. It was a nice if perilous view up there. We turned and moved up higher onto the trail. The gorge trails are not for the weak of heart or knee. They went pretty much straight up from the river, so one had to be in shape for the ascent. Sometimes the trail went up on the edge of a creek canyon. Sometimes it just crisscrossed up the hillside like we were doing here.

It was a march. And we marched quietly with our own thoughts. Since we were both knuckleheads we still smoked. Our breathing was labored. The Brittany was smarter than the two of us by a long shot so he had no trouble going up the trail. In fact, he'd race up it, round a corner to see what was ahead, and then turn around and come back to see if we slowpokes were on our way still or had stopped to gasp. Then he would turn round again and race back up around the corner. He traveled twice as far as us. I could only bark out to him that it was no fair since he had twice as many legs as me.

Halfway up we hit snow. This made the silence up there in the tall trees even prettier. It slowed us down as it was soft, and we had to stomp our way through it, me in my chic steel-toed boots. We were deep into the trees and snow, about an hour or two up the trail, when we stopped to pant. This noise emerged behind us, crashing sounds and voices that seemed odd. Who else was crazy enough to hike this route? we asked. And who was making so much damn noise doing it? It was a hiking group called the Mazamas. They were on us like a pack of gibbering children on their first time out in the woods.

The first few of them came through and identified themselves, and then another dozen or so people marched up in their conquest of this trail in unison, chattering away the whole time like a murder of crows triumphant in the treetops. They waved and chatted and bustled on. We pulled out our cigarettes, lit and held them in each of our curved hands, waiting for the silence to flow back in to fill the space between the trees. Wheaton cupped his smoke the best he could against the breeze with those skilled hands of his. We let the conversation go on up ahead until we couldn't hear it any more. Then we moved again uphill on the now quiet trail, carrying with us our thoughts about the beauty of silence, the grace of smallness, the way a hand cups itself. The song the trees make in the wind.

5

Beginner's Mind

I started. It's what you do. When I began, I was adrift in a sea of woodworking possibility. The questions were huge. How do I stand? Where do my hands go? What is this tool for?

I quit working with Harvey pouring concrete after I had lined up my first woodworking job. It wasn't quite furniture. It wasn't even built for inside. My friend Claudia now worked at a daycare center that needed a playground structure, so we designed something using logs and lumber, and with the help of Wheaton I put this assembly up.

I moved from job to job, trying to take on things that taught me something new. I built a giant sunburst-pattern wall made of multicolored cedar planks for the interior of a bead shop. It was rough if exuberant. With a partner I made gorgeous 17-foot-long strip-built canoes of redwood and fiberglass. The redwood's rich colors and subtle hues made the canoes something stunning. I had one on the water of a lake only once but as it slipped through the water I felt like I was paddling a sleek Porsche. Jobs like these were instructive and made me some money but each came with its own price. All education does.

⌣

There was a great old hardware store crosstown called Wink's Hardware. In my early days, it was in a one-story building with narrow aisles and shelves crammed full of hardware. If you needed something, the salesmen would sometimes invite you in back where the array of all things hardwarian were on display. They would take you down some dim pathway, turn once, turn again. I'd be lost. Then we would stop in the middle of a bank of boxes, with shelves filled with gadgets, gears, googaws, pulleys, drill bits, files, saws, and bolts and brass and bungs and all these things that stacked up to the ceiling, and they would pull out a wooden shelf hidden somewhere in plain sight and find the required box of widgets or wing nuts or whatnots and start to count out exactly what you needed. The store was from a very different time and felt like the best place to go look at things.

The old salesmen there were a bit crusty and intimidating to me. They must have gotten tired of long-haired knuckleheads like me asking questions. Going up to the counter and requesting even something simple like screws needed courage because I was on display to a whole lineup of customers measuring my salt. First time in I had to suffer the embarrassment of not knowing I needed a number to be served. So I was standing there, trying to look experienced, cool, and then a salesman emerged from the back of the store and looked up and called out, "Number 43?"

What? Numbers? Where was the thingee? I'm not here for doughnuts like at the bakery at home that has the numbers and all the people. I got all flustered and attempted to be calm but I hadn't noticed the number wheel, which I found hiding in the middle of the counter. I got mine and waited a bit more. The salesman finally called out a number and I piped up, "Me?"

And he came over and asked, "What can I do for ya?"

"I need some screws," I said.

"What kind of screws?" he asked.

"Screws for putting together wood." What else? I thought to myself.

He then launched into the litany of my ignorance: "Flat-head screws, or oval or round head? How about panhead? Do you want wood screws, sheet metal screws, lag screws, or sheetrock screws? Zinc-plated or stainless? Do you want brass? We have some bronze. You want square-drive, Phillips-head, or slotted? What size? A #8 or a #10? How long?"

It was an endless train of items it seemed.

He waited for the list to settle over me like dust.

I hadn't studied enough.

My feet were sweating in embarrassment. Well, I didn't know what I was asking for or what I wanted and that was that. I came to the store for help. It's why I came. Now some of the sales staff liked to push the long-haired types around, except for the one older lady whose father had started this store. She was always nice but I had just wanted some screws to put wood together and I was ignorant. I inevitably chose slotted wood screws because that must be what I needed. They were named that after all. (Note to self: These screws were and remain in fact the worst imaginable screws for any kind of work, woodworking or no. You need to drill two pilot holes, one for the screw threads and one for the slightly larger shank. Your screwdriver needs to be ground to fit the head slot so you don't mar the head, which I inevitably did. And then you have to put it in by hand, no drill gun to drive it in.) Who knew this stuff? Screws were all I wanted. Please? To build with?

⌇

I had found some cheap paperback books on woodworking. They told me a little about tools, a little about joinery. Muffie, a sweetie in college, had given me a two-volume set of *How Things Work*. This was great but mostly if I wanted to understand hydraulics or radios or power generation. I was searching for some other kind of truth. A few schools taught woodworking but they were back east and required money. There was no one in town to teach me what I wanted to learn unless I wanted to build kitchen cabinets. They may have inspired me once but they were just plywood boxes to me now, thrown together with no art. I wanted to build great pieces of fine furniture.

The craft revival was on, as was the war still in Vietnam. The Bicentennial of the Declaration of Independence was coming. Not a good time to be a long-haired hippie type with divergent views about war. I saw no need to be like anyone else I knew in school or out. I might as well have called myself a handyman or a carpenter for all that most people would understand what I was trying to do. I wanted to be a furniture maker. To me that meant that I would be a builder, a designer, a thinker.

How is it done? How do you make a life where you get to create things with your hands? That forces you to solve problems mechanical, structural, and aesthetic while putting yourself through a variety of new and strange movements in order to build something good? How do you make at least a small living at it? How do you swim against the mainstream culture that wants only quick, cheap, and disposable? How do you answer the question: Is there any value in Quality?

I would wander over to the Sears store and on the second floor I would gaze at the tool wall, wondering what in the world these things did. What sort of language did they speak? Forget language. What did these tools actually do? I couldn't afford any of them yet but I needed to know their purpose. I had no clue except what my books told me. Marking gauges. To mark what? Sliding bevels slid where exactly? Some of these tools Harvey and I had used pouring concrete, but a hammer only does one job really well. A chalk box is not much help building furniture. What about chisels? These tools did not come with a manual. They were quiet and elegant and complete in their silence.

It became clear that to do this work I would have to teach myself these new skills. Jane was my partner then and a godsend to me. A raven-haired beauty, she had the right amount of daring and nerve to stand up to me and my loud frustrations during my education. She helped me through this work while she supported us with her own job at a veterinary hospital. I had a thousand-dollar savings bond from my grandmother that I cashed in so that I could buy some tools. Jane and I also went back to that old house of my father's and to the toolshed out back, where I had played and been punished in, to get some of his old tools.

> These tools did not come with a manual. They were quiet and elegant and complete in their silence.

I had the key but I couldn't get it into the lock of the shed door. No matter what I tried, it wouldn't fit. I was getting peeved. Jane knew me well enough by then to step in and handle the matter. She got the key in the lock and promptly broke it off. We were stumped. We had to go back in disgrace to my dad and get some bolt cutters from him to snap off the lock. We finally got inside this dim place. I stared out the one window, standing at the bench with a musty tool roll of Stanley #45 plane irons in my hand. These were my grandfather's so I took them. I still have them close to my bench. Some tools of my father's I took as well since he had no use or interest in them: his old Stanley block plane, a leather-head mallet, a few chisels. I gathered up what I could, good and bad, and left that shed of memory behind.

When Joel lit out for New Zealand, Jane and I moved into his house together. He made it as far as the observatories in Hawaii. He had used the unheated garage for his metalwork, but in this three-room house there was also a basement. It had a kitchen cabinet that opened right down into it. You could crawl through the cabinet door and up into the kitchen if you wanted. Once was enough. The house had been a servants' quarters for the grander house out front, or maybe it was just a shack for someone working at the train yards close by. In any case, it was hidden by the giant blackberry bushes and the garage out front. Three rooms lined up straight together with a glassed-in doorless porch so the wind blew right through. To the right there was a stairway down to the basement. I took my dad's tools and what I had gathered with me to my new basement laboratory. It was here I retreated to teach myself woodworking. It took four years.

～

The lumberyard turned out to be no better for my confidence than the hardware store. It was in fact worse because Gordon roamed the yard where I bought my hardwoods. Gordon made my father look charitable, kind, meek, of a sunny disposition. Gordon hated my face when I walked into his yard, which was nice and neat before my ass walked in to mess it up. "What do you want?" he would say in greeting, scowling. I would tell him what I was looking for and he'd walk me down this dark-ceilinged chapel of lumber, row after row of wood stacked in great piles up to the roof. Three or four stacks high. The railroad line went right behind their building where it would stop and they would unload the cars filled with stacks of lumber right into their yard. Huge piles of wood everywhere, and I always seemed to need the stack of wood on the bottom. Which made Gordon even more cranky than before because now he had to fire up the forklift and find a spot for the other two piles and move them.

"Grab those goddamn stickers so I can put this load down."

I would put the stickers on the ground and he'd drop his double stack onto them and I'd get the heck out of his way because he might run me down with that stinky old propane-powered forklift of his. He'd park the forklift in front of the pile I was after and he would get off and say, "Well?"

Because, you see, he was expecting me to grab the board right off the top of the pile. Well it doesn't take a lot of experience to notice that the top of the pile might be good or it might be the first layer of shit. And you can't just grab off the top if you're a poor woodworker just learning and scraping by. You have to look through the pile of wood.

Gordon stared.

I stared back.

He knew. And eventually he came to know me and what I was after: The best boards I could find, the clearest with no knots anywhere, and no twist to them, and no bowing either. Better if they had terrific color and not much end checking or splitting. I simply wanted the best.

I thought I was being reasonable.

Gordon grumbled loudly when he saw me tearing into a stack. "Put it back the way you found it." He would then hop back into his forklift and motor out of there leaving me to find some other stickers to stack my lumber on and by God I would look through that pile for the three or four boards I needed. Oh and maybe one extra because it was so pretty, and if I didn't grab it then it wouldn't be there the next time. I'd pile that stack back up better than before. A time or two Gordon would come back and straighten things, jumping out of his forklift and taking another stick to slam it into the ends of the pile I had mismanaged. He also showed me how to line up one end of the pile and overlay one wider board over a narrower one, building up the pile so it was all locked together. I became neat. I became respectful of Gordon's piles of lumber. He knew eventually that he could let me look through his wood without too much bother. But it was a puckering experience at first and Gordon seemed to delight in that.

There was a lot of humility to learn if I was going to teach myself wood-working on the cheap. Still and all, those places were where I had to go and it was the education I had to get. Me and a buddy, Cameron, were at the lumberyard one time when Professor Gordon surprised the hell out of us by handing us a new lesson to ponder. He gave us each a piece of wood. Iroko, it was called. It turns out that iroko is a very hard, very pretty, chocolate-brown wood that is super rot-resistant and tears up your sinus passages when you make any dust out of it. It sends folks to the hospital with nosebleeds if they're not wearing a mask. I still have that piece of iroko. I think it was a gift.

Either that or Gordon was trying to kill us off.

"Why can't I stay up late? IT'S NOT FAIR!"
"The *world* isn't fair, Calvin."
"I know, but why isn't it ever unfair in my favor?"
—*Calvin and Hobbes*, Bill Watterson

CHOOSING A ROUTE

There was always something about me as a rock climber that wasn't right. I was too much in a hurry for an activity where you can get into trouble fast. Patience is required. Finding your way back is as important as finding a way up. There's a moral in this story here.

Wheaton, Jane, and I drove east one cloudy day to Beacon Rock along the Columbia River. We could see it stuck there like a thumb out of the other side of the river. We motored until we could cross at Bridge of the Gods. What a great name for this unspectacular caged bridge of steel trusses, but it offered stunning views back down the river. We drove along with the curves of the river until we could park by the rock near the official entry site. There was a trail with guard rails and interpretative signs. But this was not the way for intrepid hikers like us.

The three of us took off with Joe Willie leading down the west slope of this 848-foot basalt column, looking for adventure off the path. This side of the rock is made up of what is called scree. This is loose, small rock that has fallen off and covered the steep slope down to the river. It was too easy to slip and slide down and it makes for lousy hiking. Wheaton and I had this idea that we could maybe climb up Beacon Rock from this side of it.

We hopped and skidded downslope, switchbacking our way across the rocks to make it a bit easier. Joe Willie was having a grand time sniffing around for chipmunks hiding in the boulders. Wheaton and I had our heads up looking for possible climbing routes on this face of basalt. About halfway down the slope, he found a spot that looked promising. We sat and smoked and pointed at the rock, mapping out a possible path along it. Where to put our hands, searching for toe holds and finger grips, especially for him. Wheaton got started and got maybe four or five feet off the ground before quitting. Not enough to go on. Every new direction he tried petered out so he came back down. Jane wasn't interested in climbing so she avoided the disappointment and explored with Joe Willie.

I was antsy to climb. We walked down the slope a bit more. I saw a possible route and I said, "I'm going up this way." Without more planning than that, I started to climb. I got up on the basalt and then followed where the hand and toe holds led. It was good, I was moving, there was a path of sorts. It led me up a little but mostly it led me out toward the river and the base of the rock. I was going around the rock. This direction put me where the slope of the hillside moved even farther down and away from me. So after only a few minutes of climbing I was way off the ground, about twenty feet in the air, hanging on with fingertips and toes.

I realized my problem then; there was no more route. I couldn't go up and I couldn't see down. I would have to go back the way I came. I hated doing that. Backward wasn't a direction. That was a defeat. Yet it was clear that forward was no longer an option. Now I was hugging rock but my head was pointed the wrong way so I had to move my head away from the column and turn it back toward home. I scraped my nose doing it because my body wanted to move away from the rock too. There was no room for tipping backward and a nasty fall waited for me if I lost my grip. I got turned around and I tried scouting where to put my next step and hand-hold. My foot and leg started shaking on the rock from fatigue. I had been stuck in this spot for too long and my muscles were tiring. This leg dance was a curiosity, since I'd never felt it before. Once I realized that it was the precursor to a fall, it wasn't so interesting. I was in trouble.

I needed to move and got my foot over just a little. Wheaton started to talk me down. "Come back to your left. Put your left foot back down six inches and to the left. Almost, more to the left. There, now your left hand can move left. Now move your right foot . . ." I managed to get moving. My muscles started to work again. Wheaton talked me back until I got all the way to the ground. It took a lot longer getting back than going up. When I jumped down to the ground I pronounced, "Man, that was stupid."

Jane had been watching me in wonder at the spot I had gotten myself into. She wasn't going to get in the way if gravity had its way with me. Wheaton, however, said that while he was talking me down, he was planning for my fall when it occurred. He was fairly certain that I would lose my grip and hit the scree. There was nothing he could do about that. I might break a leg or something from the fall, but then I'd roll downhill and that would probably kill me on those rocks. He was planning how to arrest my tumble. No telling what was at the bottom of this hillside and he didn't want to have to carry me up.

Always practical, that guy. I appreciated that.

I got lucky with his help and made it back down the rock, escaping gravity that day. Joe Willie and I clambered back up the hillside. Did I learn anything about planning, looking forward, slowing my pace that day? Not so much I'm afraid. I was still young and in a hurry to get to someplace that sat, still unformed, on the horizon.

6

Learning Curve

Photo by Harold Wood

I taught myself many things over the years because I didn't have or couldn't find a teacher. When I was little, my brother and dad started to play chess but wouldn't show me how. Maybe I was too small still, or they didn't think me smart enough, or there was room for only two competitors—I'm not sure. I could watch. One day they had the chessboard set up but had to leave to run some errand. I sat down at the board, found the small instruction book that had come with it, and taught myself. Determination was always my strong suit.

My first woodworking machine was a radial arm saw. A more useless piece of out-of-square-do-everything-poorly-designed machine than you could ever hope to own. I thought I needed one. I tuned it so I could at least make some square cuts. Of course everything I built then was square because that's all I could do. My first goal was to build without nails or screws, although sometimes those were necessary as well. I tried to learn along the way.

Some days I woke up with a plan. Other days, most days then, I awoke too late, the dawn long gone, with a simple question for myself: "What am I going to do today?" I was free-spirited as planning was for a more formal life. Gradually I realized that I needed some kind of idea of where I was headed, goals to direct me. I needed a sense of direction for my work, otherwise I had little to show for my efforts at the end of the day.

I thought I had an idea of what a furniture maker should be, what it should look like. It looks nothing like that now. Plans are obsolete as soon as they're made because the world changes around you the very next second. Yet I think that my life retains some flavor of the image I once imagined. The beginner's mind is so hurried. He is in a rush because he sees exactly what he wants but he wants it right away. There is too much to learn, too much to grasp. Who can wait to learn? I want to be great. I know what greatness is, I want to be great right now. The beginner presses.

My marketing efforts then were limited to mostly word of mouth, friends, and some shows. In 1976 I got into a gallery, my first, with some boxes I had made, like the one little beauty I had made for Wheaton's mom. I tried selling my work in a weekly crafts show called Saturday Market. At that time, to get your space, you lined up at 7:00 a.m. on the street right under the Burnside Bridge and the organizers would shout "Go!" and you ran to the spot that you wanted. It was stupid and demeaning. I walked to whatever space was left over. I didn't think that a land rush was the right way to start a day. I set up my wares, hand mirrors and cutting boards, small jewelry boxes, plant stands. It was a long learning curve. It took me four years in the basement teaching myself before I designed and built something that I thought might be a good piece. These paths take some time to travel.

⌒

Everyone believes that accidents occur elsewhere to other people. Other people, stupid people, but not me. They think that they will always be alert and on their toes. They believe that since they have done things in a certain way for so long, then they must be safe.

"I know what I'm doing, I've been doing this for years. I've never been cut before."

There are no guarantees. Maybe you've just been lucky all this time. Every one of us who works at the bench will have an accident in the shop. There is no doubt of that. It can happen anytime we get in a hurry, forget our safe habits, or do something stupid. The questions are: How bad will your accident be? Will it be blunt force trauma or will blood be shed?

I began to collect tools and machines to do my work. I built a solid new bench for my basement shop. I still use it. A tool cabinet made of pine, built without knowing about wood movement, hangs on my wall and is slowly pulling itself apart in my shop right now. Being self-taught was a slow method of education. It took years of practice to get good at anything. Accidents occurred of course. I would cut myself in a series of two or three wounds at a time. I would cut myself on a chisel reaching for another tool in my tool cabinet. I would cut myself running my finger over the edge of a freshly planed board, or slice myself on the edge of some dried glue left hard and razor-sharp on the edge of a joint. I tried not to bleed on things.

Nothing can teach or prepare you for the first time you get bit by a machine.

That day I was in a hurry of course and my jointer knives were dull. The jointer is a powered planer with spinning knives that rotate at you. You set your wood on a metal table and feed it past this cutterhead and as it rotates it takes a series of shavings off the wood. I heard of a shop teacher who would take a broom handle and turn on the jointer and feed the broom handle straight down into the cutterhead to demonstrate its power. It was a very effective demonstration, I understand.

I was building a small walnut box, running one of its short ends through the jointer to clean it up before gluing. I was in a hurry. The knives were dull. The wood bounced as I fed it through. I pushed down hard on it to counteract the chatter of the dull knives. I had nothing between me and them except a thin ½" piece of walnut. I pushed down too much on the front end of the board as I fed it into the knives. It tipped into the cutterhead, the walnut kicked out of my hands across the shop, and my left hand was left tickling the ivories, so to speak. My middle finger got nicked by the cutters before I yanked it away. It didn't hurt. It felt more like a punch to my finger. Then it started to bleed. That's when you know it's bad, when you don't feel any pain and you're bleeding.

When you have your accident you'll immediately go into shock. Your body will shut down so that, if you can stand the sight of your own blood, you'll figure out how to bind yourself up and go get help if that's what's needed. That's what I did. I got my finger above the level of my heart, applied a pressure bandage to the wound, and watched it turn red with my blood. My stupid blood. Because that's what everyone says next: "That was stupid." Everyone who has an accident in the shop knows that it was usually preventable. It usually is. It is usually your fault. Something you did that you could have prevented by slowing down or by understanding how the machine can bite you.

I didn't know then that I needed push sticks right at the jointer to protect me. These are pieces of wood with handles that hold the workpiece in place and stay put between you and the cutters. I didn't know. I had been lucky so far, so I thought I was safe. An accident is a huge opportunity to learn something important. One takes a massive failure of common sense or logic and turns it into a learning experience. Understand what just happened and why it happened, and then never repeat those same actions again.

When you get bit by your stupidity, you have to endure the healing time of course, and the inconvenience of a bandage and splint as in my case. You also have to endure the fact of your own stupidity, that you hurt yourself. It's shameful. Why would I do such a thing to myself? This is the unspoken question. Why would I allow myself to be hurt by being careless, sloppy? I was lucky in a way with this first accident. I reacted quickly and pulled my finger out fast. I just had it bandaged for a few months. I lost the feeling in the fingertip for a while but it came back and the fingertip was unscarred. So I was very lucky. Many are not.

Come by the shop sometime. I have four push sticks now by my jointer for different lengths and widths of wood, so even if I've started a cut I can stop and grab one to finish up the cut safely. I also kept that piece of ruined and stained walnut. It's in the shop with my blood on it, as is that splint, close by my bench. I pull them out every once in a long while to remind myself to slow down.

Opportunity is missed by most people because it is dressed in overalls and looks like work.
—Thomas Edison

HUMILITY AND ARROGANCE

It was after starting this work when Jane and Wheaton and I traveled to the Bay Area for a discovery trip. On our way to San Francisco we sidetracked over to Yosemite National Park to marvel at the scenery and get in some rock climbing. Once there we drove up and away from the tourist areas and found a spot with views to distant mountains and sky. We pulled off near a clump of boulders that looked promising. It was sunny weather and a lovely spot to be in, no matter what we had planned. Wheaton figured a safe way up and around the boulders and he and I ascended. He tied our climbing rope securely to a rock, then tossed it down the precipitous hillside and left me there while he scrambled down the hillside. While I waited for him to descend and rope up, I sat in the sunshine with the view. When he let me know he was coming up, I sat on top in the sun, pulling in the slack rope, staring out at the rocks, and falling asleep with the rope wrapped securely around me to arrest a fall. Wheaton was down below climbing toward me when I heard his voice. I yelled down to him, "What?"

He yelled back, "Falling."

A conversation-stopper. This wasn't a question asking a response. Fortunately it was a precautionary yell and he had himself protected. I learned to pay more attention to things.

~

Wheaton wanted to look up old friends on this trip, Jane wanted to see San Francisco, and I wanted to meet other woodworkers. We went to the city and toured some galleries to look at work. I tried to make connections and figure out what the West Coast woodworking scene was about.

At one gallery they told me about a furniture maker out north of San Francisco near Bolinas Bay who was supposed to be an interesting character. So we headed up the coast on our way home and found his place and a sign on it that said Espenet. I had been told that since this guy's name was Art Carpenter, he didn't think that he would get the right kind of customers with that name on his fence post, so he took his mother's maiden name for his business. He built custom wooden furniture that was organic and flowing, based on wind and water and the sculpting that these elements carved into a coastline or a piece of driftwood.

I found his place along this two-lane road near the coast and saw the sign on a post and drove in. His octagonal showroom was made of darkened redwood siding and stood off by itself among the trees. It was open and I went inside. Here were pieces of Art's furniture and up high on a shelf running around the octagon were models of it. These were astonishing little sculptures really. His work was all rounded and smoothed, very organic, as was much of the work coming out of the West Coast in the sixties and seventies. His work had a richness and honesty to it that I wanted to reach out and touch. No pretensions at high style, frippery, or finery. This was work that I could imagine living with.

I looked around the gallery for a while and then heard some noise from the shop. I walked over and knocked on the door. Art was in his barn making dust and he invited me in. I had learned in the city that he had an apprenticeship program through the Baulines Craft Guild, so letting acolytes like myself wander in to make a nuisance of themselves was something he was used to.

By this time I had been to a few other shops to ask woodworkers for advice on how to do this furniture work. Jim, a friend of mine who was a carpenter then, had sent me to some guy he knew in his neighborhood, a dropout architect who had built furniture. I went to him once to ask for advice. "How do I do this stuff? How do I learn to build cool furniture?" This guy's answer was as terse, as clipped, and as useless and true as any I ever heard. "Just do it." This was the end of his advice. If you want it, you just do it. It was a cold answer, neither charitable nor helpful, and of little use to me at the time since it pointed nowhere.

Art on the other hand welcomed me into his shop. I asked about the models. He explained that he made ¼-scale models of his furniture because he couldn't draw. He used a band saw to make his curvy cuts, and it was easier for everyone to visualize what he wanted to build in model form anyway. Then he showed me what he was working on.

He was building a fall flap desk with two great clamshell shapes, one on either side. Each clamshell blossomed off the ground on two curved legs before spreading in a fanlike manner. I saw that they were made of several laminations of wood, each curved in two directions. They fanned up and out but also with a cove cut across each of them. He had cut these concave shapes on the table saw.

A table saw is designed to make cuts all day long. They are big beasts, dangerous and noisy workhorses. What Art was doing was cutting curves on them in two directions. What? When I saw this for the first time I didn't believe it was true because it doesn't seem possible. When I stopped to consider the geometry it made perfect sense. The 10"-diameter table saw blade makes a straight cut ⅛" wide through your wood in a normal straight-on cut. By coming at an angle to the round blade, I could get a round cut. (Actually two elliptical cuts from the front and rear of the blade, depending upon your angle of approach and the angle of the blade itself. Wild.) It takes some set up and practicing with small, shallow passes and a good adjustable fence. Art showed me how and more because he was using a shaped fence to cut his coves along a curve. I wouldn't attempt the simple cove cut myself until ten years down the road, but by God I imagined cutting curves with a table saw one day and that was mind-blowing.

The other tool he showed me was his router table. A router is a noisy little power tool used for making thousands of cuts. Point it in the right direction, tell it where to cut, and it will do the job. Straight lines, grooves, rabbets, dados across the grain, round over edges, ogees (an S-cut), ogees with fillets (I remember staring at a poster of router bits for months trying to learn all these different cuts), dovetails, raised panels, slotting cuts,

V-cuts. Literally hundreds of cuts can be made with the router. This was all good, and I had a router at the time, but I had a lot to learn still.

I didn't have one setup like Art's. Art had mounted his router upside down on a piece of ¾" plywood. Then he set that rectangular chunk of plywood with the router over a 55-gallon drum to catch the chips, making it the loudest router table ever invented. It worked but, my God, it was noisy. That was Art. Willing to share his bad ideas as well as his good, and a gentleman through and through. I never forgot his generosity, especially by comparison to others. He taught me a lesson that day in sharing.

It's one of the lessons that teachers have to learn, that I had to learn. That being superior to someone else in knowledge has nothing to do with your superior skill or your pedigree or your innate talent. It is study and persistence and experience that gets you to that place. It isn't just skill. It's timing much more often than not. And if you don't understand that everyone starts from a place of ignorance, if you forget your beginnings, if you forget how many mistakes you had to make in order to become the master you are, you will forget that the master needs the greatest trait in order to train others. If the master has learned well, he or she will emanate this quality. It is humility.

> Everyone starts from a place of ignorance, if you forget your beginnings. If you forget how many mistakes you had to make in order to become the master you are, you will forget that the master needs the greatest trait in order to train others. If the master has learned well, he or she will emanate this quality. It is humility.

This lesson helped me later on when I became a teacher and passed on my knowledge to other folks. In this age of digital professorship, everyone is now an expert with their right way of doing things, with rules that they find in old books, but not from their own experience. Not everyone who picks up a chisel or a guitar can show you how to use it. Even the best woodworker or musician may not be a teacher. A teacher remembers what it was like to be new at this skill. To be unsure and tentative and yet to be excited by the possibilities of this vast new world. I remember being a beginner. I remember being astonished by what I could do and yet how much there was still to know.

It was a few years after my trip to see Art. I was a young woodworker having been at my bench for maybe five or six years. I thought I knew a lot. Let me just say that right now. I had heard that there was a custom piano maker in town who was looking for some help making piano benches. Not any part of the piano itself, just his benches. He occupied a one-story building in the old industrial part of NW Portland that is now all high-rise condos, chic restaurants, and brew pubs. There he was making custom pianos one at a time in this shop. It wasn't a large shop. It holds a small bank within its walls now. I walked in and he was making pianos for God's sake. The parts were lying about. How is it even possible to make one, I marveled. He had one piano partially built on the floor.

He gave me a tour of its construction. His setup for building was impressive in its own way. We chatted for some time about this work, how long it took him to make a custom piano, the guts that went inside, the effort it took to make the curved lamination for the body of the piano, his finishing techniques to get that shiny black sheen. It was eye-opening. Truly, most of what he said about the construction of this instrument was lost on me. He had to cold-bend maple veneers to make up the sides. He had to fine-tune the fit of each cast-iron frame because they all came to him a bit different in size. In this one open room, with a grand piano half-built, sitting there as witness, he had a giant 16" table saw for cutting up great chunks of hard rock maple for piano legs and a 9" saw for precise joinery. It was an impressive sight. The encyclopedia of parts before me, the sound that had to emerge from them, the beauty of the black curvature of the piano body, the scale of the construction amazed me. That anyone could know all that woodworking, plus the sound engineering and the assembly of such a huge and elegant thing as a piano that had to be spotlessly beautiful but also sound sublime was astonishing to me. He worked alone and showed me the kind of benches that would fit with his pianos. These too would be made of maple to his design specifications. A simple leg and apron design, with a padded seat that he would get done elsewhere. We looked it over, trying to decide if I could do it. But I was stupid. I told him that I was interested in building these benches; however, I had wanted to check out the quality of his pianos first to see if his work was up to my standards at the time. I'm ashamed to admit I said something so arrogant. He was polite. After my remark I was shortly thereafter shown the door. Why bother with such immaturity?

⌒

Years later I had a student named Rich who was in my Mastery Program. His own business was laying and finishing wood floors. He had put down hundreds of gym floors, auditorium floors, private-home floors, floors for dance halls and palaces. He told me that for a time he was running a big crew of twenty or thirty guys helping him do high-end subdivisions and bigger palaces or larger gyms. What he noticed over the years was really simple and always true. He'd get a guy on his crew who had a year or two of experience and he would be the guy hiking up his pants and telling everyone how much he knew. Always full of himself, and while by no means a master floor layer, he was competent. However, his opinion of himself was sky-high, higher than everyone else's opinion of him. If this fellow lasted another four or five years, a change would take place. From an I-know-it-all position after one year, in five he was saying, "There's a lot more to this stuff than I thought. I know a lot now but I don't know near what I thought I knew. There's another whole world of things to discover."

That's the pattern. Workers go from know-it-alls, which is their insecurity talking, to a humility that allows them to learn more about their craft. As they learn what real Quality is, they learn to be open. They get to a place over time where they allow themselves to feel less than perfect. A place where they know some things but recognize that there is much more to discover. The deeper they go, the deeper it got.

Only the beginner, like I was once, can be so arrogant, lacking the needed humility. It will come, trust me. The work will teach you that.

7

The Valiant Plywood Rack

In those early days times were lean, but Portland was a cheap place to live then. Jane and I now had a house out in a rural section of town that had some newer homes mixed in with old beat-up houses like ours. My dad had helped us buy the place because it had a shop with it. Some streets around us were paved, not all. None had sidewalks. My neighbor delighted in telling me that my house had started out as a chicken shack, since I was the guy trying to keep it all standing and warm and roofed. I saw how it had been thrown up, the low ceilings of a trailer, heat vents in the ceiling, and snakey plumbing that I could access only in the crawl space. I tunneled under the house to get to the water lines. The place had a meandering floor plan with odd additions thrown on and roof lines that drained to a flat spot.

It wasn't pretty by a long shot as a house, but the shop was a decent size for me. It was made of cement and cinder block with one set of windows at its rear and a tall, open ceiling to the roof peak. The previous owner had cut out the roof joists inside to make room to work on his diesel trucks. This combination had left behind the delightful smell of diesel fuel plus the imminent peril that this roof might just slip off the walls someday under the load of a heavy snow. It had a giant roll-up door that I cut a pass door in to gain access to its greasy aroma.

I couldn't afford a truck at that time and my VW bug had been pushed to its limits as a hauler. It just couldn't carry plywood or firewood at all. Firewood was a new requirement for my shop in order to keep things warm in winter, so I looked around and found a 1965 Plymouth Valiant to use as my pickup truck. Nothing says success like driving around in a Plymouth Valiant station wagon.

Blue. My color.

It was a boat. It was a big car with sloppy steering and bad gas mileage. The brakes just worked, but that was okay because it couldn't go very fast. It had plenty of room in the back, and I actually did haul firewood with it once, driving home over a half cord in that beast. It made the trek leaning over some but it made it. I figured then that hauling stuff with the Valiant was just about like heaven would be if heaven had any taste in old cars. I put a roof rack on it and I could now move sheets of plywood. Trucks had been invented by the 1970s, of course, but I felt like I was really traveling in style.

Blue Valiant. Roof rack. Roof rack on a Blue Valiant.

My rack hung onto the rain gutters the blue Valiant had running round its top edge. These gutters had a lip on them that the rack hooked on to. I tightened the hooks down with the spring-loaded bolts that came with the rack and there it was. I could carry anything up there now.

It was a sunny day. I needed plywood for a job. I lived ten miles or so from my lumberyard, so I drove down in my beloved vehicle and bought four or five sheets of mixed plywood. All the plywood went on the roof rack, including one with a nice veneer right on top of the load. It was going to be a big day for hauling plywood. I tied my pile to the rack and took off. I was cruising down the highway in my '65 Plymouth Valiant, living the dream of independence, arm out the window, sunshine beaming down its pleasure on me.

My route home took me down a boulevard that turned from four lanes into six for a few miles. I could get the wagon up to its finest cruising speed there and make it home pretty darn quick. Middle of the day, there weren't too many cars on the road. This was a good thing. I got to the six-lane section of highway and got the Valiant up to its gallop of 45 mph. With the road noise, the wind rushing around the plywood, and the rattle of the car's extremities, I was experiencing the full ensemble that accompanied my station wagon travel. I was about halfway home and gliding down the highway in the sunshine with my plywood on my roof rack. Life was grand.

Out of nowhere, I heard this odd sound like a giant beer can being opened on the roof, a huge exhalation of air.

Ga Wump.

My load of plywood had lifted and blown off the roof of the Valiant. I had left it behind me on the highway. Holy crap. I couldn't believe my eyes. Looking in the mirror I saw all my plywood back there in the middle of the road. I quickly pulled off to the shoulder and backed up some few hundred feet with my heart pounding. There was my load sitting on the pavement. Cars carefully steered around it.

At least no one had hit it or run over it. I parked close enough to the road debris and then ran into the street to drag the sheets off the road and leaned them up against the Valiant. I rested for a bit to get my heart rate down and then reloaded them on top. The racks had lifted off in the wind because the weight of my plywood had compressed the spring-loaded bolts. Knucklehead. With that big pile on top I needed to retighten them. I was basically rolling down the highway blissfully ignorant, just being cool in my plywood-racked vehicle, thinking that everything was fine. I couldn't believe I had traveled five miles or more with nothing happening.

Other than one bent rack and some road rash on the veneered plywood, no one got hurt. My pride just walked with a bit of a limp now.

> Seeing and knowing are often separate. Nothing could be more admirable than when they coincide, but only too often they remain estranged . . . This is an obvious fact that is too frequently overlooked.
> —Soetsu Yanagi, *The Unknown Craftsman: A Japanese Insight into Beauty*

ROOSTER ROCK

Wheaton and I pursued our rock climbing in the summer months. We limited the danger because we could top rope and clip into our body harness and belay from above. At the time, this harness was like a parachutist's corset, with the same amount of requisite faith in the integrity of its parts: webbing, stitches, and ring. We would hike to the top of our chosen rock, secure a rope to some boulder or tree, and then throw it over the precipice. It was Wheaton's job to tie the knots as he knew the moves and wanted to make his hands prove themselves again. One of us would hike back down and start up the rope while the other manned it. We then securely scaled our Everest. There were palisades to scale near some rivers and good rocks over in the east gorge for us to top rope and climb up.

One day we got it in our heads that we could take on some serious climbs. We had taken the easy route by top roping long enough. Time to try some real rock and add in some free climbing and a new measure of risk. Rooster Rock is a monolith in the gorge that we saw on a drive east out of town. Once called Cock Rock for its obvious shape, it sits near the river in a beachy state park. There were some trees nearby but none grew as tall as this slab of basalt. We geared up for a climb of it by reading a book on climbing routes and how one route ran up the southern face of this vertical

49

pillar. Wheaton, Joe Willie, and I then headed out, rope and resolution in hand.

It was a cloudy day but not raining. Pretty nice day as long as it didn't start to drip on us while we were on the rock. It was a short hike up to the base. We stood at the bottom of this perpendicular shaft and got our first impression of it. It towered over us. What moved us to believe we could do this with our obvious disabilities? It rose up, almost a sheer face, with a barely discernible route across its face up to the top. Wheaton remembered this preferred route from his book of climbs. There were spikes or pitons driven in by past—and, one hoped, experienced—climbers that went up and then across the column at a diagonal up to its peak. He peered and pointed these out to me. These pitons were hammered into the rock and you and your partner clipped into those as protection, hoping that your ropes were secure enough to hold you both from plummeting to earth should one of you slip. Joe Willie was anxious to get started up the climb, but he was the only one. We stared at the basalt and tried to read its paths, imagine its perils, predict our falls.

Getting up it might be possible with our limited experience, but we had done enough climbing to know that our feet didn't have eyes in their soles. Climbing back down the pillar would be tough work because you couldn't see a thing below your feet. Blind climbing is very tough, especially when you're hugging a vertical slope like this. We considered our route for a bit longer. Cigarettes are a good stalling technique when considering things that you aren't quite sure about.

Well, about this time, two other climbers showed up carrying all this gear. We said hello and traded stories. These were army guys on leave from some base in Eastern Oregon where they had requisitioned all this equipment to come climb Rooster Rock. They had heard it was a challenge. They were prepared for the ascent. They had little red rock-climbing helmets and special rubber shoes. They each had ropes hung around their shoulders and pouches for their magic climbing dust. They had hammers and extra carabiners attached to their belts to lock into the pitons in the rock wall. They were festooned. They were ready.

We looked underdressed. I felt like we had come to the party without a costume on. Had we forgotten our masks or our pants I wondered? No doubt we were missing something of importance, and then all of a sudden we noticed that it looked like rain.

"Yep, it might rain. Could be dangerous if it rained. In fact, did you feel a drop? I think I felt a drop."

Well those army boys were better equipped than us and we didn't want to hold them up on a day when it might rain. Joe Willie was bouncing around the rocks wondering what the holdup was. Crowded rock is no good at all. Especially when it's raining out. Don't want to be waiting in line to climb a rock. No sirree.

We bowed to their obvious advantage in equipage and we took our leave to scout another smaller rock Wheaton had found in his book of climbs. We hiked to it down along the railroad tracks and scouted it and decided not to climb it either. Dear Prudence. We were learning.

8

Expectations

Photo by Harold Wood

I always brought hope with me to the exhibitions and craft fairs. I thought that someone would finally recognize my talent and keep me busy for a lifetime. A patron who would understand how I needed to be supported, hail me as the genius I was, and then life would just be floating downstream.

Perhaps my expectations were set a bit high.

This particular furniture show was held at a small museum for the forest industry called the Western Forestry Center. This was a very nice wooden building with exhibits and movies about logging in Oregon. Fine furniture makers like myself had set up around the hall. That first year we were all upstairs on the second floor, displaying our work for sale.

A remarkable event occurred. I was standing silently with my furniture arrayed in front of me. Standing, smiling, no venal sales techniques for me. No inviting everyone to sit on my stools or look at my cabinets. No working the crowd, getting their phone numbers if they were interested. No, I would let the work speak for itself. It would sell itself.

As my work was generally mute, we made a good pair. Two strong silent types.

Selling was never my strong suit. People would come by and if they liked a piece, they would appropriately Ooh or Aah or say nothing at all and move past. This particular show however a gentleman approached and took a look at my cherry tea table and he nodded his head.

"Hm, hmm," he said.

I had no witty retort ready for this, so he repeated himself with a twist, "Hmm, hm."

Again I was speechless in front of him. What to say? I waited.

"Hm, hmm," he said yet again. "I see that you finish like I do."

Okay, he had me. I hadn't said two words about my finish on this table. Not a word yet he knew that we two were kindred spirits. I listened on. I was his captive audience.

"Yes, you finish just like I do."

I crumbled under his attack. "Yes, do I?" I asked. "How do you finish?"

"Well," he said, "I spray on lacquer because that's the only finish to use. You know dust is a real problem with lacquer so the first thing I do is empty out the spare bedroom. I take out all the furniture from it, and then I vacuum the drapes and I vacuum the floor. It has to be spotless. I have a sprayer, you know, so I spray on the finish and I want the room clean so I vacuum everything. Walls, drapes, floor, and then I mop the floor once to get any remaining dust gone, and then I bring in my spray unit and I make sure that the canister is full and that the tip on the spray gun is clean—and I can test that outside, which I always do, I always test it outside before bringing it in—but then I have everything ready inside this room. I have the spray gun and can filled and ready, I have the furniture on a revolving stand inside, I have the room made spotless, and then I strip down to my socks and my underwear . . ."

And that's where I stopped him.

"Nope. No sir," I said. "No sirree. I do not finish the same way as you, sir. I do not."

He was a bit taken aback, I could see, by this news. Stunned perhaps by the vehemence of my reply, he was made silent by my denial and maybe even hurt by my pronouncement.

"No sir, we do not finish the same way," I said, "because I do not spray on lacquer for my finish. No sir." He was surprised at that bit of news, expecting that he and I were just alike. I told him that I simply oiled and wet-sanded the piece with 400-grit sandpaper to get my glass-like finish. Whether I was in my underwear or not I left it to him to decide. He retrieved this startling information about me and moved on.

Expectations, gentle reader, expectations must be controlled. They must be handled firmly or they can crush hope. Manage your expectations for your own happiness.

This quote comes from that notable humorist, the Dalai Lama.

Choose to be optimistic. It feels better.

MOUNTAIN SIDE

Up on the mountain was a different kind of air. Wheaton and I had decided that to really get a sense of it we had to be out on the mountain in winter. Now at the time, winter gear was pretty decent if you liked carrying an extra twenty pounds on your back. Extra clothing, parkas for cold, parkas for rain. In an Oregon winter you were as likely to get rained on as snowed upon. So we carried woolens. Our skis were wooden then and we used wax on their bottoms to help us get through the sludgy snow. Our packs held extra socks, sleeping bags, tent, camp stove, and as much food, chocolate, water, and cigarettes as we could carry.

We had decided to drive up to 6,000 feet at Timberline Lodge on Mount Hood to start our hiking. It's what the mountain climbers did. This seemed a more prudent approach than starting at its bottom, like at Klickitat Falls. Even if we were only going to spend the night it was worth it to start up as high as we could and light out from there to see how far up we could go. We signed in at Timberline Lodge at the Wilderness check-in and headed out to the snowfields and started walking.

Wheaton was familiar with this place of course. It was up here on the mountain where he had been working on the ski lifts. This was where his accident had happened, up at Timberline Lodge. How this affected him

being here, I did not know. He didn't talk about it much once he had healed. If it bothered him, well, he was going to walk straight back into the mouth of the beast to confront it.

～

Maybe what had happened was not so much of an accident after all.

I had known Wheaton in school as a motorcycle rider and racer and a general smart guy. His career as a scientist was less certain than what I saw for others as he wasn't sure what he would specialize in. He was a year behind me in school. We liked each other and would hang out and go out for beers at Lucky's Tavern. When I punched in the front end of my VW Bug, staring at some girl on the sidewalk as I drove along, he helped me fix it by crawling into the trunk to work on the lock. My friend Jim would tell me years later how Wheaton came up with a method—because he was without all his tools—for setting the timing on a truck motor using AM radio static. Solid guy, great with his hands, and he loved to fix things.

His last year in school I was back in the Midwest. It was during the semester break that year that he had been driving his girlfriend Wendy in her Volkswagen back across country. It was in Utah where it happened. He had fallen asleep at the wheel and lost control of the car, totaling it and putting Wendy into the hospital for a long spell. She came out broken, walking twisted, and feeling very angry if alive. Wheaton went on but it must have plagued him. He went to work up at the ski lifts on Mount Hood after graduation. It was a job. Maybe it kept his mind off things. He and Wendy split up.

Wheaton's job up on the mountain was in maintenance working the chairlifts up in those old drafty sheds, taking care of their cables, greasing them, making sure they were in good repair. The ski lift is a powerful machine capable of running its 1" steel cable at 8 feet per second and carrying over a thousand people per hour up a mountain. The lift cables of course have to be lubricated to keep them flexible and rust-free while pulling loads of skiers thousands of feet higher. They're under incredible forces of tension and compression while moving their loads. Then they have to roll around the giant bull wheel drums at either end of their trek and head back. They have to be strong yet supple and able to withstand sun, wind, rain, snow, and freezing cold temperatures that may all occur in a single day. There is constant maintenance being done to keep them whole and functioning smoothly so the skiers never notice them.

It was decent work and Wheaton always liked being outside, being up on the mountain. Out in one of the machinery sheds, the 100-horsepower diesel motors were always noisy with lots of clatter. The wire ropes wrapping tight around the giant drums would make it hard to hear yourself think. Gloves keep your hands warm in the cold on the mountain but around moving machinery they're also an invitation to get them yanked into trouble. Gloves give away your sense of touch. Maybe Wheaton always wore them on the mountain. He had to know how close to danger he was. He was greasing the cables that day and wearing gloves around the thick moving lines. Why else would both of his hands be so close to the moving wire rope? It must have been part of the job that he enjoyed, being so close to something so powerful, so dangerous, so elemental. He must have felt at risk but alive.

> It was a moment's lapse of concentration. A fluke, a turn of the head at the wrong time, a movement of his hands towards the beast, a sound that made him flinch, and in that instant it changed his life.

It was a moment's lapse of concentration. A fluke, a turn of the head at the wrong time, a movement of his hands toward the beast, a sound that made him flinch, and in that instant it changed his life. One minute he was whole and the next minute he was changed. He got both his gloved hands caught in the drum that turned the ski lift cable and they got pulled under the steel wire as it wrapped around the drum on its way back uphill. It crushed his hands as he watched and tore off his fingers. I don't know how he got his hands out except by pulling them out in a panic. The wonder of it must have been stupefying. How could this have happened? Take me back just one moment in time, Wheaton must have thought, just one click back.

When this kind of accident occurs there is the first pain, of course, but then the body shuts down into shock so that the pain disappears long enough for you to protect yourself. His body numbed so he could move away, escape the monster, run, collapse, stop bleeding. There was nothing of his hands to be found to put back on.

He went into the hospital for a few days while I was still back East. His hands were bandaged up for months. I cannot imagine what that waiting for the unveiling must have felt like. In the mid-1970s, hand surgery was still developing. The surgeons did what they could for him, but there was nothing to sew back on. There was no magic to make his fingers reappear, no prosthetics to replace his missing digits. Wheaton had remaining only an askew little finger, a bent thumb and forefinger on his left hand and some stubs. He had roughly the same combination of mashed and missing digits on his right. His hands were cross-stitched versions of their former selves with space where there should have been fingers. Both his thumbs remained at least and that left him able to grip a tool.

$\backsim$

Jane, my sweetie, and I took him under our wing sometime after the accident. One or two of his fingertips stayed bandaged for several months. Eventually all the wounds closed over. The fingers would stay bent the way they were for the rest of his life. They held themselves open into a kind of tensed grip like they had touched something too powerful, something we are not supposed to touch.

We had him over to our little house to sit and have dinner with us and talk and smoke, play cards, drink a beer or two. It was good for him and good for us to have him around. Jane and I took care of him because he needed to heal—not just his hands but also inside. We helped him find a way back and he came back hard, changed of course, but he came back hard and made himself a life. As I look back on it now, it seemed to fit a little into what I was doing at the bench. There was something about his way back that inspired me.

That's when we started hiking together and rock climbing, and everything that I did he did better with a few working fingers and a thumb on each hand. Still and all there was something about Wheaton that I could see would always plague him. Maybe he would deny it. Maybe it was my Catholic sense of guilt projecting onto his tragedy. I think that he had never gotten past what he had done to another human being, Wendy. I think he had allowed himself a moment's stupidity and this was his punishment for his mistake, the one that had changed lives. And yet it was still an accident, one that he rescued his hands from. How could someone so skilled have put them in harm's way like that?

It was a move so final and catastrophic that he would carry this stigma with him for the rest of his days. It was a sign that he could show to everyone else that he had sinned and here was his punishment. He did this with a kind of pride too. It was strange. We would be somewhere together and meet somebody new and he'd stick out that mangled paw of his so fast, as if to say, "Here it is, you're gonna look at it anyway, look at it now. And in fact, touch it. Shake my mangled hand." And it was something to grab, I can tell you.

When I was a little guy, my father had a business associate named Terry come over to the house from time to time. We would always shake his hand as we were trained to be polite. He was missing the first part of a middle finger. Maybe it had been taken by a saw or a car door. Some mayhem had gotten it. It didn't matter how. He had a gap in the coastline of his fingers that made me stop and stare, as much as I didn't want to.

Now here was Wheaton and the stubs and fingers on his two hands were barely able to hold and light his cigarette. He was burning to be more capable than two of me and usually proving it. He constantly pushed himself to see how far he could go with only some mangled fingers on each hand. He accepted it. Maybe at some level he was at peace with it because he had faced his own disaster head-on. He showed me by his example how to survive. He was my hiking partner.

〜

The mountain can be clear as a bell up here during the day. I looked up to the peak and saw the Palmer Ski Lift headed up to about 8,000 feet. It looked so tiny with those little metal columns stuck into the rock like lawn ornaments lined up the mountain. The clouds can be gathered below at this elevation or they can close up around the mountaintop. We headed up a distance, carrying our skis and packs. We made it up almost as far as the Silcox snow hut before I started to get a bit mountain sick. This is a nauseated feeling caused by altitude and not pleasant at all out on a glacier. We turned around because I had no desire to get higher up the mountain. We skied down the western side of the giant empty snowfield. Even two neophytes like us could snowplow our way down safely. It was glorious. Although we were at a steep part of the mountain, we skied at a gradual decline down the hill and then turned around and skied back across slowly and then turned around again in our slow descent.

Which is when I lost the ski.

I stopped on a steep slope and slipped a little in my cable bindings. Off the ski went downhill. A frightening thought came slow to me. At first I was upset that I had slipped the ski. As it left me and started to pick up speed, I realized what a perfect machine it was for gliding down a hillside. A fantastic design, slim, sleek, fast, gone. I saw that it was picking up speed and I thought that I might lose that ski forever. There was nothing I could do but watch it. I might be walking back home now. I waited, hoped for a faraway sighting, and then I undid my other ski and started downhill. Maybe I would spot it. I trudged through the snow downhill before I found it. I got lucky as it had hit a mogul a few hundred yards down and flipped over and stuck in the snow.

I skied more carefully then. We still veered off to the west away from the ski lift and headed down and out toward Mississippi Head. This was a cliff face we wanted to view from a distance, not encounter in the light of the setting sun. We skied down to an elevation we thought was good and then skied around the girdle of the mountain at about a consistent elevation until we felt we were far enough away from errant travelers but not too close to the cliffs. There on the side of the mountain, we pitched our tent and waited for night.

Snow camping requires a certain suspension of the idea of comfort in exchange for a breathtakingly cold beauty. It is a curious mixture of pleasure and pain. I walked along the snowfield and watched little bugs scurrying along on their errands to do something. What late-night feast were they headed to? I looked out from our tent site on the round edge of the mountain with a view some 50 or 75 miles to the south and west, with Portland off in the distance. It felt like I could step off into the sky. Nothing to do but stare out at that distance. Or look up at the mountain. Either view made me feel small. I tried to keep warm in my smallness.

Food takes on a different meaning out here. Food wasn't food here; it was fuel. Fuel that kept us alive. We set up our tent facing into the sunset. We shook out the sleeping bags and put them inside. I got out my big Primus stove and fired it up. Wheaton made us a gourmet meal of freeze-dried mashed potatoes, with chunks of cheddar cheese and ham thrown in just as the potatoes got hot. He stirred the freeze-dried potatoes with a spoon and his gloved fists and at just the right moment the piece de resistance. In a minute it became cement. It was such an appalling meal to choke down that Wheaton came up with a name for the dish: Peristalsis Interruptus. It was like glue cooling so quickly, this viscous potato pudding that cooled too fast in the frozen mountain air. It tried to close off our throats. We swallowed, we warmed it with our mouths and ate it, and then aglow in the victory of our survival, we smoked some cigarettes and ate chocolate in the rarified air. Not much better chocolate than some eaten at 6000 feet. We were alive again.

In the middle of the night, I had to get up to eat again as I was freezing. My motor kept burning up fuel so I had to eat some trail mix to keep warm. I put on my snow booties, a warm essential, and walked out onto the snow-field to see the night sky, the lights of the city far off, the dark of the forest edged by the white of the mountain above and around me. It felt like I was at home in my slippers, with the cold turned way down, looking out a picture window at the black sky, the white mountain, the dark trees. It was worth a lot to be out here and able to see this. Captured in a picture in my memory and nowhere else. I still have those snow booties. Those are worth a lot to me. Not too much later I made some drawings for a wood sculpture called *Peristalsis Interruptus.*

9

The Magician Distracts

There was an event that brought many furniture makers together for the very first time. It was called a confabulation and was held at a crafts school in town. There was some fine furniture work on display at the show and tours of larger shops and talks about the craft and how to survive in the field. It was great because it got us reclusive types out to meet one another. We had the opportunity to exchange techniques and concerns, get fresh ideas and perspectives.

One woodworker whose work was on display in the show came from Montana. Turns out that this guy, Steve Voorheis, knew my brother, who was teaching now at the university in Bozeman, and so we met and chatted. He had built this incredible armoire in mahogany, six feet high with carved art nouveau double doors, a dovetailed cabinet with exquisite details that just knocked me and everyone else out. It was the star of the show. He and I got the chance to talk about work and design as we hung out one afternoon. I took him to see a large outdoor cast bronze sculpture that I loved, and it was great sharing ideas about design. I also marveled about his craftsmanship on his piece when he said to me, "I should show you something. When we get back to the school, let's go to the gallery. I'll show you something there." I was intrigued. Show me what?

We drove back to the other side of town and the show. Steve and I walked past the front reception desk, through the gift shop, and then up to a railing that surveyed the gallery floor below. I looked down at his magnificent piece across from us. We strolled down the stairs with the sensuous carved hand railing to the main gallery space, filled with pieces of beautiful furniture. He took me up to his amazing armoire and I stared at the front doors, its magnificent presence, and then Steve quietly took me round to the side of the piece. He pointed at the dovetails up on the top right side.

He said, "Look there."

I looked and saw nothing. I said, "What?"

He pointed and said, "I screwed up. Look there. I screwed up and cut all my dovetails on the wrong side of my lines. They were all off and I had to patch them. I fixed them all." And sure enough, when I got up close and looked very carefully at the joints there were the patches glued in. But they were almost invisible. I had never seen them. I was stunned. I was so busy staring at the amazing doors and the carving and the sensuous shaping that I had only glanced at the dovetail joints.

The magician had done his work and my eyes were diverted from the mistake by the magic in front. I only saw the beauty of the piece. It also didn't matter to me. It never matters to another woodworker if she or he loves the form, the shape, the feel of the work. No one looks for errors then. Mistakes are human. I loved that Steve had showed me his fix, let me see behind the curtain. It was good to see this trick even if I didn't know yet how to employ it yet.

All art is failure.
—Richard Hugo, *The Triggering Town*

THE PENCIL

A stroll across the shop can be an adventure too. How many steps do I take back and forth in search of a tool or scrap of wood? It offers a glimpse into my psyche, watching myself move about the space trying to save a step or two, circling to go from one machine to the bench, from one stack of wood to another.

I believed this day that I was on top of things. I had my act together. I was busy working, getting things accomplished, had all my ducks in a row. Maybe the job was late that day or maybe I was trying again to get too much done at once. The deadlines closing in on me. There was always so much to do.

I walked past my table saw on my way to turn the corner of the saw and head for a pile of lumber on the planer. A No. 2 pencil was in my hand. I rushed past the saw and swung my right arm up and the end of the pencil hit the bottom of the table saw table. The rubber eraser stuck to the table and the pencil pivoted and spun around and the sharp point jammed into the palm of my hand. I stopped in my tracks. I felt something. I picked up my right hand to stare at a No. 2 pencil sticking straight up out of my palm, like a flag planted in a newfound country.

All by itself.

I was stunned. How could I do something like this? How was this possible? Straight up the pencil stood. I was amazed. It hurt some of course, but I couldn't believe my feat. I stared in disbelief at my hand for a short time trying to understand the unlikelihood of this event. Then I pulled out the pencil.

Shake my hand sometime and ask to see the spot in my palm. The graphite lives there still. I had to tell myself again to slow down and focus. The signs were clear. "Slow down. I'm in a hurry."

I yam what I yam.
—Popeye the Sailor Man

ACT TWO:

PRACTICE

10

A Hundred Shoes a Day

Mastery has no endgame, I discovered. It is a goal of course. Yet there is no turning point felt and reached. There is no singular moment when something happens and all becomes clear. Of course we who work with our hands consider becoming a master. A master of wood, of clay, or paint. A master of welding or hammering metal into shapes, mastering the violin, the fiddle, the bow on the saw. However redolent the smell of the goal of Mastery may be at the beginning to an acolyte, it doesn't seem real once you get down to the work of the thing, the practice of it. Then it's just your striving every day to get better while staying alive. It's a ghost, this dream of Mastery, a phantom that gets in the way of the work. I can't be striving for Mastery if that's all I'm thinking about. Who can say when Mastery will appear, when it will shine on someone? The thought occurs that I will have to survive long enough doing this work for me to become a master at it. Mastery then is for someone else. Let me do my work.

Leave me alone, desire. Leave me to my work. That's how it is. I worked. I paid attention to the work. Everything else happened along the way while I wasn't noticing. I worked with tools to make my furniture and my living.

There was one tool that did change my life in the shop and I had no idea how it would influence me and my building. It was a machine. One machine shaped my world, changed my outlook, tuned my sight and sense, and it was the one that helped me become a master. It was a bandsaw.

After my first years of teaching myself about design and how to build things with carpenter's tools and my radial arm saw, I began to realize that the world of furniture also had curves in it. This was a revelation to me. Everything I had built up till then had been straight. Straight cuts, straight lines, sturdy, well-made, and straight as an arrow. When I saw what was possible with a curve, I felt like a baby child learning to stand. Everyone else around me was standing; they knew how. I was a bit slower, but I had discovered something about curves and their appeal. I stood and looked around at the curved world differently then.

I started searching through the want ads in the papers for a lathe. I had heard about them of course back in college. You made bowls with them or baseball bats or other round and curved things. I didn't know what all I could make with them really, but I started to look for a lathe to change the shape of my work.

I found a band saw instead.

It was an old 16" Yates American band saw. Industrial green in color, it looked like a large, green cast-iron plug on four legs. It stood there dumb and silent. Perhaps it was I who was the dumb, silent one. I didn't know what the saw was about or what it could do. Some guy had it in his shop in the house that he had built and he was done with it. I had never heard of the Yates American brand. And the 16", I learned, referred to the diameter of the two wheels of the saw. So it was a midsized saw. Your butcher has one that's around 14" in diameter, made of aluminum so that it can be hosed down and cleaned every night. Band saws also come much larger. I saw one once at a boat-building school that had 36" diameter wheels. I walked up onto a platform to approach this giant. It was 7 feet tall and was used for cutting 30-foot-long curved ship keels.

A new machine in the shop, like my new band saw, has a presence. Woodworking machines aren't usually tall. This one was tall. It stood a little under 6 feet in height. It stood purposeful too, filled with the promise of . . . something. I wasn't sure what just yet.

It was made of cast iron with art deco–styled doors. The table could tilt to make angled cuts. It had a rack-and-pinion fence that I could move over by dialing a knob and locking it down to make straight cuts. That was reassuring to me. Thin, welded blades ran round and round the wheels so I could cut straight but also cut curves, depending upon the width of the blade used.

The seller wanted a good chunk of change for it at that time. I negotiated a little and got thirty-five bucks knocked off the price and I took it home. I got the original brochures from him for this Y-16 as well, which said that it was a school shop band saw. The saw came apart so I could carry the cast-iron legs downstairs to my basement shop and then the motor, the table, and finally I got a little help to get the main body of it down my stairs. I put it all back together and then stood back a few steps and leaned against my bench to take it all in.

What was there to learn about this new green beast? All these questions came to mind that I wanted to ask it. What can you do? The saw was quiet, just standing there. I flipped the switch on it and, after a bit of delay, a few seconds of ascension, I could hear the motor wind up to velocity. There it was, running. Now what?

The rest of the saw was fairly simple. All the force of the blade went down into the table so there were no kickback issues like with the table saw. There was less wood wasted with each saw cut because the blade was narrower. Keeping your fingers away from it was the most important safety thing to remember. I could rip up lumber safely and accurately with the fence on the saw. I dialed the fence in to where I wanted the cut, locked it down, and with patience made fine cuts.

> Do you want to cut fast or do you want to cut straight? You can't do both.

This opened up a whole new world of woodworking for me. I could cut curves, circles, ovals, and straight lines, and make rip cuts along the length of a board or resaw wide boards into narrow veneers. I could cut up a small log on this band saw or make fine joinery. It wasn't fast like a table saw. A blade engineer asked me once, "Do you want to cut fast or do you want to cut straight? You can't do both."

A lousy band saw is what most folks first buy and they're mystified hearing from me that the band saw is the most important machine in the shop for a furniture maker. Their little 14" saws won't cut straight. The cuts can wander off-line or belly around the wood if pushed too hard. A bad saw will drive you to misery. Isn't it a poor craftsman who blames his tools? Isn't that how the saying goes?

There is a difference between a fiddle and a Stradivarius violin. And there is a difference between one saw and another. A craftsman can do adequate work with a poor tool but he can compose symphonies with a great band saw. He can build work not possible with a bad saw. Yes, I was lucky and got one of the heavyweight saws that was loaded with cast-iron to dampen vibration. I kept a sharp blade on it and slowed my feed rate down so the teeth in the blade had time to clear out the sawdust in the cut. There was no need to adjust for blade drift by angling the fence. With a sharp blade and the weight of the machine, everything about this saw was simple and honest. Built so that a farmer off in the boondocks somewhere could fix it himself. Built to last.

All kinds of shapes started to appear in my work. The curves of the legs of my tea table appeared. The shape of my stool legs came from the band saw. I could now make tenon cuts with ease or take a wide board and set up a tall auxiliary fence on the saw and, with a fresh blade, cut through the thickness of that board and make two wide but thinner boards that I could glue up into a book-matched panel.

I also learned that I could make money with this saw. After we had moved to a new house and shop outside of Portland, Jane and I now had a bit of land to stretch out upon. Down the road and across the creek from us was a lumberyard. I got friendly with the guy running the yard and he hired me to cut wheel chocks for someone in the railroad. These chunks of wood are shaped round to fit under the wheels of a car to keep it from moving. He asked me if I wanted to make 200 wooden chocks, cutting them to a specific circumference from 4×6 timbers. I had my new band saw so I jumped on the job. I would haul these 8-foot chunks of 4×6 fir back to the shop, cut them up on my radial arm saw to length, and then take them to the band saw. I made curved cuts in them over and over again, one after another, staying close to the line I had drawn. I had one try to get these cuts right. There was no going back and fixing the shape if I wanted to make money. Cut it right to the line the first time. I must have done a thousand of these chocks.

The job did several things for me that were far more important than putting money in my pocket. It taught me how to saw, how to saw accurately to a line, and how to be patient and listen to the motor work. I could watch the blade cut and know when it was getting dull, or when it made a sound that said that blade might break soon. I learned to listen to the sound of the motor when it complained during a cut, when the backside of the blade rubbed too much against the wood. It taught me to be patient.

Slow down, I told myself again. It helped my sawing technique in so many ways, this practice, this repetition, this patience I had to learn.

Some years later, a famous sculptor in town hired me to cut up shapes on my band saw for wooden maquettes of his very large steel sculptures. He asked me if I could cut to a line accurately. I smiled just a little and said yes, I can cut to a line. He was surprised at my confidence. When you have the knowledge in your hands, the confidence naturally comes with it.

I still have this band saw close to my bench. When I moved to a new shop up on a second floor, I moved the band saw close to the good natural northern light coming through the windows. It was close to my jointer so I could use the two together when rough-milling my lumber. This saw was as symbolic a tool as any I owned. It signified my way of being in the shop, solid and precise, flexible, able to do so many different jobs for me and do them well. It was my lucky day to have found the Yates. It changed my work and helped to define my path.

When I started holding classes in my shop space there, I would always tell my students this very important bit of safety information: In case of a fire, the alarm will sound, and the auxiliary lights will come on, which will point you down the hallway and out to the stairwell. Now don't panic as the lights keep the pathway well-lit and there will be plenty of time to get down the hall and to the exit. Follow the stairs all the way down to the ground and follow the signs outside to safety. You will be on your own. Move calmly and quietly, but don't panic, as I won't be leading you. I will be dragging my Yates American band saw on my back outside with me.

The person who helped me was a big helpful man in his late fifties and, making conversation while he looked for the parts, he mentioned how good our weather has been. "We'll be pitching horseshoes this weekend," he said. "The kids will be bringing the shoes and stakes." I told him that I had had an uncle with cerebral palsy who couldn't talk well or walk well but who could pitch horseshoes with the best. "Isn't that great!" he said. "You know, I had an uncle who was tri-state horseshoe champion three years running. I asked him one time how I could get as good at it as he was, and he said, 'Son, you got to pitch a hundred shoes a day.'"
—Ted Kooser, *Local Wonders*

DAISY PLAIN

It had been a few years since Wheaton and I had gone up Abner Ridge to scale the mountain. He had left town to go work for a British trekking company that ferried tourists by lorry across Asia, Africa, and South America. Wheaton had a few months before his first trip and met up with my friend Jim, who was on his way to build a house for his sister in New Jersey. Jim said to me once, "I have a photo somewhere of me and him building the house. It always seemed like the hammering turned his broken hands into bloody stumps. He never griped and was always cheerful. He was a quick learner and was fun to work with. He stuck around until it was time to head off to Africa."

Wheaton acted as driver, cook, the inevitable mechanic, and the continental guide leading these treks. This seemed suitably odd, challenging, and exciting for him. I myself was busy at the bench trying to become proficient at being a furniture maker.

I had come back to that forest near Klickitat Falls with Joe Willie, my Brittany spaniel, with no high hopes to scale a mountain like before. I drove into the flat river-bottom area called Daisy Plain off the High Pass Road. The road was a bumpy dirt one for a few miles. This was before the forest service paved it. Back then it was a more isolated spot and you had to know at least a little about driving around roots and holes and boulders in the road. Nowadays the most important thing to know is to hide your valuables in your car. I parked on the side close by some other vehicles, trying not to block someone coming out.

The hiking was easy enough at first, walking through the flat sandy area to cross the river. Once I got to the old bridge over the river I had to be careful. It was simply a wide log set over the river with no handhold. When the water was running high in the spring the rush of it, the gargle of sound over the rocks, made me fine-tune my attention. No slipping allowed here. All my focus was on staying upright. I watched my feet when they were close to the water like this. In the late summer like now, when the water was down, if I kept my eyes a bit higher and walked across the log bridge like it was any old pathway, I crossed it easy. Joe Willie and I headed up the trail.

It was not steep, meandering close along the north bank of the river at first and then moving into the trees above it. The bottom area got broader and the river noise quieted. It was a good place to let my thoughts wander alongside me as I walked. Once in a while on the trail I'd get a view of the mountain through the trees. Just a glimpse of some snow on the heights and then the trees would hide it again, closing in around me. I walked on looking at rocks or the trees, deciding where to plant my foot in the trail, just there between two hemlocks, and push off and keep walking, make a choice, turn here, step on that rock, avoid that root, put my hand on that small fir. Each decision about where to place a foot happened quick, moving along like the fluidity of time with no stopping, just movement. I let these choices flow into my walking reverie, like the screech of the scrub jays as they followed above me through the trees. There was only a gradual rise in elevation as we walked. My tempo was determined by each footstep. The trees were short and scrawny here, young and plentiful. My thoughts kept pace.

I hiked with Joe Willie still racing ahead of me and then rushing back to check on my progress. At the spot of the old forest service guard station we had a choice of heading on to the falls or taking another trail away from them. What was down this fork had always made me curious. We dropped off the main trail down into the river canyon, into the bottom area where the ground flattened out and there were only a few trees. According to the map this trail existed and it went back across the river and on up the mountain's southern side to a somewhere I never found.

Down here in the river bottom there was a grand view up to the mountaintop whenever the clouds cleared. A volcanic mountain like this one, so close and towering above me, was hypnotic. My thoughts went up high and distant to the snowfields and far away with my sight, and then they would come resounding back to me when I remembered to hear the river rushing by or saw a dipper flying by upstream close to the water. I tried to imagine what life was like here once. Maybe it was always this open and rugged. The trees were gone from this flat area so there was sunlight and space. Who knows how many years ago and how many times some rush or catastrophe of rockslide and water had come roaring down the mountainside and scoured this place out? It was the reason for the broad plain and the size of the trees along the trail. I spent some time here imagining a future as rugged and open for myself.

I had come to my woodworking out of a desire to recreate myself, to become something new. The expectations of others were no longer my concern. I didn't have the same need to be perfect for them, to satisfy their requirements. I wanted to be in charge of my own future. At the same time, my move was one away from university politics with its world of petty rivalries and machinations for power. I didn't want to worry myself with those elusive goals and the intractable standards of academia. I had seen enough. Watching others work in a corporate world also convinced me that I didn't belong there either. Woodworking was an alternative life of solid if solitary work. I could pour myself into it because there was so much opportunity for creating and so very much to learn. What got done in a day's time sat before me on the bench. The evidence was clear and tangible. It was a challenge that I could take on with no standards but my own.

That was part of my problem. I carried the disease of perfection beat into me by my father. However much I spurned his approach, his lack of empathy, or his anger, I still had this ridiculous and powerful urge to please him. His idea about perfection was that it still wasn't good enough. I could always do better. So I had impossibly high standards to work toward, an urgency to get good and get good fast. Plus I was my own teacher.

I went to the woods to understand my choice as well as this need for perfection. Look around, I told myself. This was a fine place to be. It could not be improved upon, with the view of the mountain up above me, the river tap dancing over the rocks next to me, and the sun smiling down on me. Yet it was a jumble of bushes and rocks and water. Where was the need for making it perfect when its beauty came from its wild qualities? This standard of mine for perfection made me strive to do really good work, but it was crippling because it slowed me down. I needed to get out from under this burden that I carried with me while still improving my skills and learning the business.

I liked being down in this river bottom. I walked up and downstream, boulder hopping and enjoying the openness of the place. Good place to be with the dippers and my thoughts and my dog. I walked the river, pacing my jumps between rocks, then stopping to stare up at the mountain. Good views to be seen from here.

11

Don't Do It!

I remember hearing a famous wood-worker once say that he'd never ever had a problem with one of his chairs. Never. Hmm, methinks someone was spinning tales. Things happen, and they happen to everyone. This is not a condemnation. It is simply a fact. It's just marketing blather if someone proclaims how perfect their work or their life always turns out to be. The only question is whether you buy into the myth.

One other point to note—and I mention this now to students who enlist the aid of spouse or partner or friend in the execution of a glue-up—apologize in advance.

Gluing is one of those maddening detours into a new time/space continuum. This is where time speeds up as the universe, my bench, goes flying off into a quick orbit around whatever solid object in space I'm trying to assemble at the time. Distractions do not exist, noise ceases, the birds stop singing as if a full solar eclipse was in process, time rushes past me at the bench like the shadow of the moon across the ground. Too fast, too fast, but there's no time for complaint as the glue is more inexorable than that moon. It will recede very soon so I must keep on track, stay focused—there is only the gluing for us here. All my clamps are ready, my mind is made up to finish this job, my assembly cauls are near at hand, I have practiced, I have helping hands. Oh, I'm sorry if I yell at you if things go amiss, forgive me in advance for screaming at the inanimate objects in the room, help me through to the other side.

It was a stool glue-up for me. Hours and hours of prep work coming down to five minutes of sheer anxiety, the final glueing. I had cut all the joints, made the rails for the compound angled legs, fussed with their fit, glued and wedged this whole undercarriage of legs and rails together. Now it was time to glue on the seat. I needed help for this glue-up. I called on Jane to help me. She was brave. She came out to the shop.

This stool design has four splayed legs. Sticking out the tops of those legs are tenons pointing in toward the center of the seat because of the compound leg angles. Everything on these legs points in toward the center of the seat. Which means that the holes drilled into the seat for these tenons are angled as well. These angled holes are farther apart at the bottom of the seat than they are at the top. That's what these angles do. They move things closer or farther apart.

The leg tenons were then closer together at their ends than the seat holes were at the bottom. So to get the seat on, I had to stretch the legs apart without breaking anything and bend the rails, bend the legs, pull them apart until I could get each tenon started into a seat hole. Once in place I grabbed my rubber dead-blow mallet and beat the hell out of the seat trying not to break it but also trying to get that seat down onto the leg tops before the glue dried. But the mallet was not enough, it was never enough.

Once I got the seat started in place, I needed clamps to pull it down completely. I had them ready, along with wood clamping blocks to protect the seat from the steel pads of the clamp heads. This is where I needed Jane's help, in setting those blocks and clamps in place. She was brave.

I had the glue in the mortises, I had the seat started onto the legs and banged it down as far as I could with my dead-blow mallet. Then I put a clamp from each leg bottom up to the seat, where I needed the wood-clamping pads. She held them in place for me. Once I had the clamps on, I cranked down on those as quick as I could to pull the seat down. Four clamps on each of the four legs together putting this almighty pressure on things and it had to be done evenly and quickly. I had done this before so I know it worked. But *this* time, on this lovely walnut stool, this time as I was clamping down on the seat, I got the seat down evenly to all four of the legs but the bottom of one leg, where a clamp was pushing too hard against it, gave way. It split the wood and the clamp fell to the ground with a clatter, but with the seat in place and the corner of the leg cracked off.

I was stunned. I was destroyed. All that work ruined.

I couldn't believe it, after the hours I had put into the build. How could this happen to me? What did I do to deserve this kind of torture from the woodworking gods? Hadn't they done enough to me, made my life hard enough without more problems? I had my answer. I got angry. I knew how to make this glue-up end. I grabbed the walnut stool. I threw the clamps off. I raised the whole assembly over my head and I was ready to smash it to the ground. I was filled with indignation. It seemed at the time righteous and so I felt bidden to do this because it was my right and I had made this thing and it had spurned me at the very end, it had turned against me and now it was time, it was time to show it. I raised the stool over my head and I was ready to pound it down to the concrete floor to finish it off, to exact my retribution.

Jane yelled at me, "Don't do it!"

I stopped. I looked at who had spoken. It was Jane. I shook my head. Was this a stool over my head? A walnut one. I knew this piece; I had spent a lot of time on this stool; I put it down. What a raving idiot. I set the stool on the bench and breathed a little. I looked at the broken walnut of the leg. I found the piece of wood that had come off the corner. I picked it up and saw that it fit back onto the leg perfectly. I would glue it on later.

What had happened? I had my consciousness again, and I calmed. It was a setback that looked bad yet it was minor. I ignored it for now and glued and hammered the seat wedges into place and set the stool down to dry. I apologized to Jane.

༄

Come over sometime and ask to see the walnut stool. You won't know by looking at it which leg it was that I fixed. I'm not sure I even do now without careful examination. What came from that accident was a new method for attaching my stool seats. It is a simple plywood clamping jig that works wonderfully and has yet to fail.

What a lesson. When problems occur they suck up all the air in the shop. They are gigantic, cataclysmic, insurmountable. I was lucky that day that Jane was there to yell some sanity into me and bring me back to a normal time and space. If you do not have this life preserver nearby, then quickly walk away from the problem. Walk away and let it shrink back to its normal size so a solution can enter the room.

These are the inventors, the engineers, the designers of the
world . . . to these intrepid pioneers of purpose, a failure of any kind is
not so much a disappointment as an opportunity.
—Henry Petroski, *Success through Failure*

ANGEL'S REST

Living up just past the forty-fifth parallel makes for long summer days and
longer winter nights. The lights shut down early in the fall months, especially on cloudy days. It was a gray Thanksgiving that I spent at my friends,
Robbie and Marilyn's house, eating too much and feeling it, lying there on
their couch. We had stuffed ourselves early with dinner in the afternoon
and were on the couch in a haze. Their dog Hershey, the chocolate Lab, was
beating everyone and everything to a pulp with his exuberant long tail. I
got a wild hair and announced, "I'm going for a hike. Wanna come?"

Robbie and Marilyn were made of sterner or saner stuff than I. They
looked at me with curiosity and little interest. I didn't want to be a slug
on the couch, and there was plenty of time for a little hike to go work off
some of the effects of the turkey. To my mind, it was only about three in
the afternoon, time to get somewhere. I thanked them both and got in my
old sports car and drove off fast heading east out of Portland down the
Columbia River. No rain threatening. Or perhaps rain threatened all day
but it stayed put in the clouds.

Angel's Rest is the first real hike I think of when heading into the Gorge.
It's trailhead has moved through the years. I used to have to walk down the
road a piece before coming to it, and it was hidden in the ferns and vine
maple off the side of the road. Folks used to drive right by it all the time.
Now there are big signs and mileage listed and a map and the parking lot
can handle too many cars so the trail will get worn down. The state still
hasn't determined how to encourage while discouraging folks. My car was
the only one there this Thanksgiving afternoon. I started up the trail. It
begins at a nice pace down in the trees and ferns paralleling the road for a
time. Then it heads up in a hurry and that's no surprise, even for these first
hills of the gorge. The trail usually took me an hour or so to walk up so I
started moving quick in the fading light.

The noise of water alerted me to a creek up ahead. There were falls I could
just see, and then the trail came upon the footbridge over the water. It was
here on another day that I remembered stopping to stare at the wet black
stones near the creek. I thought then, as I stared at my round, distorted

visage, that this was the first looking glass that anyone ever held. This day I walked on by the bridge moving up on the trail. It went out and around the hillside before hitting a couple of slides of scree littering the hillside. It was bare enough to see up and out to the river. Lots of small rocks on the trail, so I took care walking, moving slow across the open patch of slope. Then I was back in among the trees, dark and damp and close in to the creek again. I could hear its sound as it moved by.

More switchbacks and the trail stayed on the northern slope of the hill for a time, hitting a tougher section of exposed ladder-like switchbacks, one after the other, gaining me elevation in a hurry. Then up near the top the trail wrapped around the south side of the hill, hitting a big bare patch of boulders. If it was clearer I could see back down toward town. The trail switchbacked again, and then I was on the big rocks right near the bowl of the cliffs. I got up on top of a ledge for one of the prettiest views of the gorge, looking east through the obscuring clouds.

That's when someone turned off the lights. The sky went dark.

⌐

It's true. I was on the cliffs when the lights went off like a switch had been thrown. I admit I had rushed to get to the top of the hill, but once there I wanted to have a look around. To savor for a moment my effort and what the world looked like from up there that gray Thanksgiving day. That's when someone in the sky said, "Okay, that's it for today, shut 'er down." And the lights went out just like that. I couldn't see a thing.

It was black. It was night. I was an hour away from my ride on a cliff. I had no flashlight.

This could make someone feel pretty stupid for rushing into the woods. My argument was that I was escaping gluttony and lethargy, noble causes on a cloudy Thanksgiving day. I managed still to feel some kind of stupid up there. My decision to go hiking was laudable but I hadn't considered the downhill part of the trip very well. I wanted to get up the hill in time, which I had. I simply hadn't expected the nightfall to be so complete.

My safe return was important so I started walking back the way I came. I realized that I wasn't completely sightless at first, at least up on top. There were no trees covering what little moonshine penetrated the clouds. I managed to negotiate the exposed rocks until I was in the thick of the trees that hugged the north hillside.

There's always time on a hike for contemplation, even meditation. I was full of questions for myself, like why hadn't I noted each turn, each twist of the trail? Why hadn't I taken notes? Why hadn't I remembered my way up so I could go back down it in the dark? This part of the hike down was when it got really interesting because what I had to do was move slowly down the trail and feel with my foot in front of me to determine where it was. The situation was too dangerous to permit me to get mad at myself for putting me here in this spot. I was here so I had to deal with it. I kept telling myself to slow down. A step off the trail toward the river would put me over the hillside, and I didn't want to spend a night banged up down in some brush or broken forever on the rocks. If I kept at it slow, everything would be just fine.

The blackness of a forest makes one alert of course. Lions, tigers, and bears, and all that, but the added weight of being able to fall down the steep hillside added an undercurrent of anxiety that was hard not to notice. I had to put my fear aside to focus on what needed to be done, which was movement on the trail home. Shut up and move downhill and be patient, both with my pace and with myself. Admit to the accusation. Case closed, verdict in, I was an idiot. There was no doubt. But I also needed to talk back the fear.

I stared hard, trying to see in the dark. My feet were only barely adequate as trail indicators. I looked for signs of blackness, signs of emptiness to my right, which indicated a pitch down the hillside. There was nothing to hold on to from the hillside of the trail except my balance. Then I started to spy light on the trail down at my feet. I wasn't sure if I was hallucinating or if I saw what I saw. Little dots kept appearing. While they were too small to light my way, they acted still as a kind of guide for my feet because they seemed to be on the trail. That is, if these were really lights. I didn't know what they were. They would appear and disappear. Were my eyes playing tricks on me? Were these bugs? Was my intense staring causing me to see spots that didn't exist? I didn't forget the jam I was in, but for a time I thought this was a cool hallucination or a rare time for a manifestation of luminescence in the forest. This kept my mind busy off a tumble down into the darkness. It helped to calm me.

The weather was mild and the rain hadn't started, so I kept inching my way downhill. I eased down the exposed switchbacks, knowing that there was the river way out there somewhere. I moved past the two or three slides of scree with no incident, making sure to lean toward the hill side of the trail and feeling carefully for the path. Rock on a path in the dark feels surprisingly just like rock in the daylight, so I searched for the rock underfoot that seemed flatter. At times I knelt down to touch them, to steady myself and to find the curve of the trail. My path in the trees felt different, the blackness closer. I could sense that. Out on the slide of rocks, the blackness moved away from me. There was more open air, less pressure. The sporadic road noise from beneath me served as another balance point in the night. I leaned away from the noise, which was downhill, as I could feel the cliff's pull. After some walking the steepness of the pitch lessened and the trail became softer underfoot. I was touching more dirt now and less rock. My fall now would be less precipitous. This at least was an improvement.

The good in my situation was that there was no hurry for me. The light was already extinguished so I wasn't rushing to catch any sunset. The rain had held off. It took a few hours but I limped down the hill this way. I got to where the trail evened out a bit, the steep hillsides all fell away, and the ferns grew high. With no fear of falling, as I was off the hillside now, I felt the pressure release. My walking became a real pleasure as the trail was easy to follow. I picked up my pace to the parking lot, where I found my car. I was happy not to be spending my evening out in the woods. The night did have its own kind of light and sense and feeling, and I was glad that I saw it. I was in some way satisfied that I had put myself in that spot and then gotten out of it. I had received another lesson about hurrying. I had also learned something about relying on myself. I had walked back down the hill alongside my patience and my fear. Quite a pair to take a slow walk in the dark with.

12

Discipline and Practice

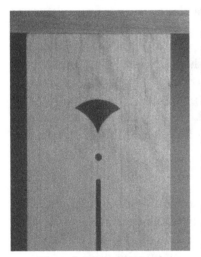

Photo by Harold Wood

Not everyone wants to practice. Not everyone has the discipline necessary for practice. If you are skilled or want to learn something, it is the only thing that allows you to get better and to develop your skills. Most people do not want to practice. They just want to be good right away. They want to skip the work part and just be great. It takes discipline to become skilled.

My father taught me discipline. A Catholic high school education reinforced it. I was taught that if I do a job, do it well. To those two stern teachers I owe a debt of gratitude. I learned to work hard and that is the most valuable thing I ever learned at school. It wasn't the biology or the literary symbolism or theories that were critical. It was the discipline that was the most important. Forcing myself to work when I didn't feel like it. Getting to the bench to get a job done when I wanted to play. Learning to focus when I wanted to dream. Practicing denial of some pleasures in order to get something back in return. It is a paradox and the repayment can feel slow in coming. It is there over time if you have the discipline. Discipline is what I used to become skilled.

The dominant cultural paradigm that we are sold now of living faster, buying more or bigger or faster, is not for me. That's one way to live. There is another. To slow down. To try to do your best work. To make your efforts count. My father taught me many things that made me punish myself for not being good enough, but he also taught me that valuable attitude about doing the job right.

There is no shortcut to Quality. It takes effort. The hard work is part of the reward. If you dedicate your life to mastering your skill—and it will take that long, if you decide on this journey—then once it is inside of you nothing but your last breath can take it away from you. To fall in love with your work is the key. It is never work then. Always strive to elevate your craft and to make your work better.

It did not come easy, learning at the bench. Because that sort of discipline requires patience, and patience was never one of my strong suits. Plus our furniture work is labor intensive. It can take a week to finish a piece, or a month. This need for patience in how I design, how I consider my steps in building, patience in the shaping and preparation of my wood, patience in the application of hardware and my finishes. This is hard to learn. It takes time. "I want it now." Slow down, I'm hurrying, I have to remind myself. It is frustrating. It does not come easily. When it does, when my work flows from a place of calm and is not hurried, but paced appropriately, what a difference is felt. Maybe I understand a little where this mastery comes from.

∽

Some of your discipline can come from external sources. I used deadlines as a motivating tool. Here's the job and here's when it needs to be done. Deadlines helped me focus. Your own education is personal. Your desire to improve your skills has no contract to sign off on. This drive has to come from within. I wanted to build better work that was designed with intention and made well. So my discipline, my desire to improve, was based on an idea of where I wanted to be and what I wanted my work to look like. It wasn't much of a carrot but it motivated me. I had this imperfect notion of what a furniture maker and designer should be building so I took on jobs that helped me in this. I was the one in charge of what I would create. The only issue was finding people willing to support me in this goal. In other words, clients.

Here's a story of one of my pieces. I had spent four years underground in my basement shop teaching myself how to build. When I started to build bigger things, I wanted my designs and my work to be better, so to practice my skills I would build things for the house. I designed and built a coffee table out of red oak because the wood was cheap and we needed a table. This project also gave me the chance to learn about hand chopping my mortises with a chisel, which was something that I felt I needed to try. Now this is slow work and I needed to pay attention to get those walls of the hole, the mortise, clean but also straight in and parallel to one another. I chopped and I sharpened and I sharpened and I chopped my mortises into this red oak, and I cut my tenons with hand tools and my band saw. I fit the joints together and made a nice-looking table base. Then I glued up boards for the top, cut a groove into the top rails, and glued my top into those as I assembled the whole table and put some finish on it. And there it was. Pretty nice work I thought.

Months later, I looked at this piece and saw something terrible. One of the joints on the top had split open at one end. It had delaminated. This was no good. I couldn't call myself a woodworker if my work was going to crack up. If I was selling this work, I would have to move every few years to keep my reputation on the run. This minor disaster made me consider what had happened.

I realized first that wood movement can pull even a glued joint apart. I had glued my top into the rails and they hadn't allowed for the wooden top's movement. Listen to your house throughout the seasons. Listen to these cracks and pops during the evening hours. This is wood movement in your furniture, your cabinetry, maybe the house itself. When my tabletop tried to expand or contract, the table base tried to prevent it from moving. Something had to give. It was my glue joint in the top that popped. I learned how to make better laminations using something called a spring joint and I learned to pay attention to wood movement from then on. I had to keep my standards high even if, as a self-taught woodworker, I didn't know what the standards were. I figured that in my field, a reputation lay in the results. I wanted everyone to know that they were getting my best work from me.

> What's the point of doing work that no one will appreciate, no one will recognize, even if I point it out to them? The answer is simply that I will see. I will know.

After a time though the issue of economy will come into play. It's tough enough surviving as a craftsman in this world. Why keep up high standards? What's the point of doing work that no one will appreciate, no one will recognize, even if I point it out to them and show them the intricacy of my joinery, the dexterity of my hand tool work, the brilliance of my design. Who will care? Someone may say, "No one will see this extra work. Why do work that no one will know about? Why put all this extra effort into it?"

The answer is simply that *I* will see. I will know. It will be me who knows that I did my best work, imperfect though it usually is. This is not the road to riches or fame but I have to let go of that desire to be rich, let go of the desire of fame. Do the work for myself. It takes discipline to do this. I have to recognize that some of the time spent on a piece will never be compensated, the client will never know what I've done, and even another woodworker might not notice the care taken over the smallest detail. Yet over time my value as a craftsperson will show. I will be compensated over time both for myself and when others start to notice. If you are the kind of maker that takes care, you will be found.

↭

Here's a story of someone taking care.

Sonny Rollins, the jazz saxophonist, became dissatisfied with his sound in the early 1960s. He quit doing gigs and practiced instead on the Williamsburg Bridge in New York City for months to perfect his sound. He did this without accolade, without compensation. He did it to get better. Who would know? Sonny Rollins went on that bridge to practice because he knew that he had to be a better player. He knew that this practice would make a difference in his playing and in his life. Hadn't the great Charlie Parker in his youth spent twelve to fifteen hours a day practicing in order to get better at the Kansas City jam challenge sessions he frequented? Sonny Rollins had to practice. And now late in his life he can think back with no regrets and say to himself, "I did this. I made this happen. I made the sacrifice and I did it for me and it made me who I am this day."

There is no price that can be placed on this willingness and on this knowledge. No cash value that can be counted out in your hands for this type of satisfaction. You do this work because you have to do it, for yourself. Practice this and good things will come from it.

Twyla Tharp, the modern dancer and choreographer, in her book *The Creative Habit*, talks about the importance of ritual for an artist. Whatever form, be it an odd form like cleaning your room, a mystical form like lighting incense or unfolding a dollar bill, whatever mundane form it may take, that ritual signals the beginning of the process. And the practice is an important part of the ritual for a woodworker. Because the work is so labor-intensive, there are so many jobs to perform well, it simply takes time to learn the steps of each to master them.

Practice is the key. If you can learn the discipline to practice, one day you will surprise yourself by how much you have learned, how much you have taught yourself.

Some years later I was making library tables for the new state archives building in the state capitol. It was an important job with a design competition that I had to win in order to get the contract. With this contract came a lot of responsibility because the architects also gave me the design of the cabinetry to be built and installed. Designing for the state library, I was meticulous in how I wanted the tables to look. I went to other libraries around the state to do research. Not in books. I went to look at the library tables themselves. I went to different colleges and universities to see how their tables were holding up over time. What worked best for materials and design? I went to my old college first but the tables there had recently been replaced and so they looked great. The old ones that were still around were made of oak and were quite stout and solid, Gothic in taste.

The tables at the local city university were not designed well nor particularly well-made. Form is function is boredom and they were good to sleep at. The tables I visited at the library at the Mount Angel Abbey, designed by famous architect Alvar Aalto, were veneer over plywood, as were the library counters. These were designed by someone famous and so they must be done right, yes? Not so much. They did not fare well as there were wear spots at their edges. Places where elbows and arms had rubbed through or where books rubbing over the surface every hour of every day had worn them out. So much for veneer as a surface material. They were worn and shabby instead of gleaming with age and the polishing of use. I wanted my tables to grow worn and beautiful over time.

I decided on several details after my research. The tables would be all solid wood. They would have structural elements that would also be design features that would help to prevent racking and swaying over time. They would be built to last. They would have some details of the architecture of the building in them. I used the curvature of the library walls as a starting point and added that into the shape of the tabletops. I also wanted something in these tables to rest your eye on. A detail that would help your mind wander. I designed a pattern based on a pine cone seed's shape and planned to inlay that into the tops and end columns. If I used solid wood for the tabletop, I also had to make sure these joints would hold. This meant cutting spring joints for the laminations as I could not have these joints fail.

Spring joints are a technique for ensuring long-lasting edge laminations. It is a simple concept but can be difficult to accomplish, especially on long boards like I had. My tables were seven feet long. What I wanted to have was a slight concavity along the edges of each two boards being glued up. A little bit of spring to them where the boards touched at their ends, but in the middle there would be a little space I could just barely see some light through if I held the boards up to look. In this way, when I applied my clamping pressure and glued the boards together, there was extra pressure at their ends and all the gaps closed up along the lamination. There were seven or eight boards in each of the ten tabletops I had to make. This made for a lot of spring joints to cut.

I had a helper at the time and his work was adequate but it was showing too many gaps in the joints. He argued that the joints he was producing were within industry standards. I said to him that I didn't care about the industry. My name was going on these tables and they had to be right. It was frustrating not to be able to get these edges cut right the first time. We worked on each joint until it was just right. Then the top would be right. It was worth the extra effort.

My preferred signature is modest. My initials carved into the bottom of the tabletops sufficed. It's better sleeping weather when I know I've done my best work.

You don't make the work, the work makes you.
—Steven Bogaerts

THINKING BY WALKING

I have no solid evidence. This is merely my hunch, my speculation. I came up with this theory while walking. Simply put, movement is important to thought.

The pace of walking is suited to our way of thinking. It is the rate at which we are supposed to be thinking. I believe we evolved as animals who climbed trees, who strode across the prairies, who walked from one camp to another, one fort to another, one city to the next until we learned to ride on animals, on one another, or on conveyances that were conceived by great and lazy minds on their walks.

Read Wendell Berry's *An Entrance to the Woods* to understand the important of pace. "Our senses, after all, were developed to function at foot speeds; and the transition from foot travel to motor travel, in terms of evolutionary time, has been abrupt. The faster one goes, the more strain there is on the senses, the more they fail to take in, the more confusion they must tolerate or gloss over—and the longer it takes to bring the mind to a stop in the presence of anything."

Walking is connected to thinking. This pace is one of meditation. It is the time for us to move ideas around as we move through a multitude of sensory stimuli. It is playtime. It is not considered remunerative so it is frowned upon. Yet daydreaming is not wasted time. It is enormously powerful, if scorned and misunderstood by logicians. Our brain is still mysterious ground for us even given our accumulation of knowledge. Consider your own dreams, if you can remember them from last night.

The pace of a walk helps call ideas forward, unlike driving or riding a bicycle. I had a student who used his bicycle as his only form of transportation. In the worst weather he cycled, even if walking was safer or drier. On ice, in driving rain storms, he rode his bicycle so he could get There. Wherever "There" was, he wanted to get there faster. That's one way of traveling. I know that something is missed by those cyclists, drivers, and commuters whose minds are set on getting there: wasted creative time.

> Daydreaming is not wasted time. It is enormously powerful, if scorned and misunderstood by logicians. Our brain is still mysterious ground for us even given our accumulation of knowledge.

The meditation that can be walking allows my crowded thoughts to sift their way through my consciousness. They work themselves out in ways that are not logical or sensible. It is a place where synthesis must occur. This is creative right-brained activity and not logical left-brained work. This occurs in a locale where our mood and the colors and smells along the way, the shapes we see can all contribute to this synthesis and perhaps to an idea of merit. We walk and we dream, and then we put these dreams into action.

Walking acts as a curious stimulant to my brain. It opens me to a world of sights and smells and sounds that by its tempo, its rhythm, its curiosity finds fresh combinations and remembered patterns. I hear melodies or I play a song over and again in my head. I regain memories or bury them under new ones. Being on a long walk is akin to attending the symphony. A friend of mine once told me, "It's okay, listen to the music and just let your mind go wherever it wants to." I use this same method when I walk. I try to have no conclusion to reach when I set out. This is simply an opportunity to let things sift. Like my beagle and his nose used to do, I let my mind take me wherever it may.

⌣

This right-brain activity, then, is very much like dog brain activity. It is not linear; it is synthetic. It is not logical; it is intuitive. It is not temporal. It is always in the moment. Time flies when I'm on to some intriguing idea. Richard Feynman was a Nobel Prize physicist because he allowed his brain to put together regular ideas or facts in new and unusual patterns. Not logical thinking, even in a field as reasoned as physics, but holistic creative thought.

· When NASA's space shuttle *Challenger* exploded it was due to a massive failure in team communication, understanding, and in simple O-ring gaskets. Feynman determined the cause for the failure with a simple synthetic experiment. He showed the presidential commission on the disaster that a low temperature could compromise the integrity of the gaskets by changing their shapes. Freezing temperatures had occurred the night before the launch. The O-rings compressed and failed to seal, which caused gases to escape, blowing up the rocket.

Feynman showed this in an embarrassingly simple display. He put one of the O-rings in a glass of ice water with a C-clamp on it. When he removed the clamp, the gasket failed to return to its original shape. This lack of integrity after a freeze/thaw cycle would have allowed the gases to escape, causing the explosion. By thinking out of the box Feynman reproduced the failure that NASA failed to acknowledge and many other scientists could not determine.

Jill Bolte Taylor was a neuroanatomist, a scientist who studied brain activity. In her 2008 book *My Stroke of Insight*, she talks about synthetic brain activity from her own experience with a stroke. Her inability to use the logical left side of her brain after her stroke allowed her to see how domineering that side was. With her left hemisphere no longer active, her ability to organize things in a linear fashion left her. The detail side of her brain, the descriptor, the narrator, the *I am* that scheduled her life was shut off. Her stroke allowed her access to the right side of her brain and its nonlinear way of thinking. The shift from a linear process to one of impressions with blurred and blended edges left her with insight into her creative brain. Creativity required that she put the linear aspect of her brain aside long enough to be playful and open to all possibility with no judgement, no need for perfection. With no path to follow, everything had some value then and was worth exploring. She could discover new syntheses, new ideas, and new forms that both sides of her brain could then develop.

⌇

I need to put myself into a different frame of mind to be able to create. Movement does this for me. Walking sifts ideas, images, and inferences working through me into action or mood or choice. What I see at this pace is easier to hold onto than when flying in a plane or riding in a car or on a bicycle. Time slows down for me, and I never know what conclusion I may reach or problem I may solve. The very act of walking helps me to process. It doesn't always yield results. It sometimes gives answers in a completely different arena with ideas popping up unbidden. It's illogical yet fruitful, which is why it's so intriguing.

In *Zen and the Art of Motorcycle Maintenance*, Robert Pirsig wrote about how the French mathematician Poincaré made several important discoveries after walking. Poincaré felt that his "subliminal self" had helped him to feel his way to a truth by discarding rules, by eliminating unnecessary ideas and letting the solution rise up to consciousness. This is the same concept that Pirsig's character, Phaedrus, refers to as "preintellectual awareness." Only the interesting and useful ideas break their way into consciousness. Twyla Tharp writes about how walking stirs the brain: "Movement stimulates our brain in ways we don't appreciate."

All artists need to stimulate their brain somehow. Action is the tool that uncovers ideas for me and opens my mind to possibilities. Walking, then, works as both meditation and stimulant. Think by walking. Thoughts, ideas, patterns will emerge that seem to come from nowhere but are created in the fine sifting of our experience and senses.

Creativity is the residue of time wasted.
—Albert Einstein

13

You See It?

Photo by Harold Wood

If you build things in wood, I know who you are. You love tools first. Your hands are drawn to them. Tools have magic in their grip. They hint at their potential, about their capability, their promise, the power that lies in holding them. It is something old and atavistic, something real with smells from decades ago, these tools that you love.

The second thing is that you adore wood. It's hard not to because it's so gorgeous and warm and malleable. It feels good in your hand. You can shape it, bend it, lay down gorgeous, thin veneers of it, or smooth it to a sensual form that is inviting and warm. It wears and weathers over time, becoming even more lovely as it is used. I believe it is as essential to our being as the other elements. Wood gives us heat and hearth.

Number three on my list is that you're a problem-solver. You like to figure things out for yourself, find your own solutions. It makes you feel good to come up with your own way of doing things, your own path to the conclusion.

Fourth, you need to know where everything is in your world. You need this sense of control in a world that's gone mad. Where is my hammer, my piece of wood, those screws I bought? You need to know where you put things and that they are there because the world is a crazy place and you need to have some sense of security that where you place things is where you will find them. So you create for yourself a shop space to work in, a bench to work on, an atmosphere that makes you feel good when you walk into it. A place where you know, roughly, where everything is. My own bench is a mess most of the time. Sign of a superior intelligence is what I say, because I know that my tools and drawings and templates are all there, somewhere.

The fifth reason for being a woodworker is all the hats that you get to wear, the sheer complexity of it, the number of jobs required to build a piece. From the designer to lumber buyer, millwright, joiner, assembler, and finisher, the number of different tasks is impressive. These skills are appealing because for each one there is so much to know, to assimilate, to master.

Finally, and perhaps the most important reason that people become woodworkers, is that you need to talk to yourself. You need to be alone so you can converse with yourself throughout the day. The importance of this cannot be overlooked. It is crucial to our mental health. It may seem maniacal to others to see you chatting to yourself at the bench. This is the time to be quiet, the time to recharge your batteries. Perhaps it's the best conversation of the day for you. You need to have a decent chat, one at least in a day, where things make sense and the call and response are logical, not crazy like the world trying to blow itself up, not insane like the news, or counterintuitive like corporate decisions to close down factories and ship the work overseas because it's cheaper.

There is a certain amount of healing that also needs to go on at the bench. This is your time spent conversing with your history or working out the day's issues, coming up with new designs or plans as you work on a project, working out a new way of being in this world.

There you have it: a portrait of a woodworker. A lover of inanimate objects, adorer of wood, a puzzler, controlling, quiet, thoughtful, and he talks to himself. Very close to the image of a crazy person you don't sit next to on the bus—but let that go for now.

These woodworkers are also stalwarts that can be depended upon to do what they say they're going to do. They keep their promises to build you something. Their problem is that they can't tell time and have no sense of reality when it comes to considering how long a project might take. A weekend project is an euphemism for "Next month sometime." I'll get to it soon, really means, "I'll get to it after I rebuild my table saw and move that lumber rack and fix my crosscut sled and buy the lumber and think about that project for a while." They will get it done, eventually. Patience is an important quality to have with them.

One other trait that woodworkers have is that their focus is incredibly tight. It has to be in order to create such marvelous work. It is not like carpentry where sometimes ¼" is close enough. In the world of building furniture, our tolerances are as close as the thickness of a sheet of paper. I tell my students when they're planing a board with a hand plane that a dollar bill measures four one thousandths of an inch, 0.004" thick. Their shavings need to be half that thick, 0.002". It gives them a sense of perspective. When doing inlay work, it is measured in one thousandth of an inch, 0.001", maybe less. With this very tight focus, our vision tends to get myopic. We see errors, faults, defects in our work, problems, mistakes, catastrophes, ruination that others simply do not see.

I tell my students about my woodworker friend Michael. Some years ago, he and I worked in a building that had once been part of a huge furniture factory. It housed then about a dozen small woodworking shops up on the second floor. It was a great space once you found it through an underpass of the freeway and across the railroad tracks and then went upstairs and got inside the door of my shop. It was built in Sullivan's Gulch before the freeway came and hid it away. Built long ago when a train spur ran through the back parking lot to unload lumber and load up furniture. Michael had a shared space with a view of the freeway south while I had great northern light on the other side of the hallway and a roof that leaked whenever the sun came out. The tar would expand and the water on the roof would snake its way into my space. Dumb idea to make a V-shaped roof in Oregon but there it was. I had a gutter inside my space. Over the years Michael and I would help each other glue up, talk about designs, and lift many heavy objects together, both physical and spiritual.

I would be working on a project and run into a situation where something felt wrong with a piece. Something to my eye looked off and I needed confirmation of this fact. It could be a dent somewhere or a patch, a misplaced hinge. The mistake would occur and then I had to decide if it was obvious. Was I being too harsh, too critical? Was it me or did I need to launch into the costly fix? First I needed another set of eyes to confirm what I saw. I would call Michael over and have him look at the piece.

I would ask him, "You see it?"

He would respond, "What?"

"Look at it," I would say.

And he'd say, "What?"

"You don't see it?" I would ask incredulously. I was starting to doubt his ability to use his eyes.

"I'm looking. What am I supposed to be seeing?" he wondered aloud.

"I can't show you. I want you to find it. Don't you see it?" Perhaps Michael needed glasses, I thought.

"No, what? Where?"

"C'mon, you don't see it?" And then to myself, It's as big as life, it's staring right out at you. You don't see it? It's right in front of you.

But I would not say this. I would not point it out. And again Michael would say, "I don't see anything. What are you talking about?"

"It's right there. See?" And then I would point at the offense, the insult to aesthetics, the blow to the senses, the crime against virtue, the single greatest visual catastrophe that a craftsman has ever committed. There in front of his face. My finger pointed down to the sin.

Then he would say, "Oh, now I see it. So what?"

I was stunned. He didn't see it like I did. He never saw the mistake like I did. Never. This scenario reenacted itself enough times for me to understand that my mistakes, the ones that looked so huge to me, were often things that to other eyes, even professional eyes like Michael's, would look just fine. He wouldn't even stop to look at them, or if he did see them, think nothing of it. Sometimes I did wonder about Michael's willingness to look critically at my work with the great seriousness it required. There were my mistakes sitting there so large and visible, and I needed confirmation of that. Just look.

The same was true for his mistakes. He would have me look at his work with a careful eye too, and I would never see his errors like he did. It is never as important for the observer, for the client even, as it is for the maker. The maker whose ten-thumbed approach,

> My mistakes, the ones that looked so huge to me, were often things that to other eyes would look just fine.

whose blindness and incompetence, whose woeful lapse of concentration has caused this flagrant violation of all design and construction principles. That maker. That idiot. No one sees it like him. No one is as hard on his efforts as the builder.

Bear that in mind as you look at your own work. Step away, sir or madam, from that piece. Step away. Put down the hammer you are considering to throw. Put down the hammer you want to take to this work and step away from the project. Try to see it with someone else's eyes. It's not so bad. You do pretty good work. It's worth remembering.

> He liked having a drawer, it was a neatness you could see just sliding it open.
> —Pete Dexter, *Deadwood*

Birthday Hike

On the other side of the Columbia River the hills climb up and away, scattering apart as they move north. One hill juts back toward the river, leading with its chin. It's called Mount Aaron. This birthday I needed to be walking alone with my thoughts when I started up this familiar trail. The ascent gets your attention right away as it moves up quickly, hugging the hillside. The trail is broad and well-traveled at first as lots of folks come here for the view.

My birthday hike tradition had started some years ago when my sweetie at the time decided to leave me the day before my birthday. Something about finding herself with another man. I had trouble hearing what she was saying over the roaring noise inside my head, although I understood her words. She told me that she was leaving and then asked me if I wanted a party the next day. I decided against that gesture and instead began my tradition of solo birthday hikes.

I had reached a cleared swath that crossed under the giant power lines hanging over the trail. They came from downhill and close by Bonneville Dam, which I could see down to from here. Maybe it was a mile or so away as the line flies. There was even a bench for viewing the expansive river plain and dam. The hillside was cleared of trees for the towers and power lines, which climbed up over the hills and took off for points west like a team of horses. I looked east down to Bonneville below me. I turned only slightly to see to the top of Mount Aaron. It was tree-covered along most of its base, but then a precipice of rock grew up from those trees and stuck out its jaw toward the river. I always wondered at how I would walk all the way up that rock.

The hike leveled for a bit now as I moved around the hillsides. There was a good-size creek that appeared quickly, although I should have remembered it. There were so many steep hillsides and canyons, the water had to make itself known in a dramatic way. The waterfall had a bridge just under the spill of it. There was a secondary trail that went up if you wanted to get close to see the falls. Being below it on the wooden bridge was enough for me. It made me stop for a time, staring at the boulders taking the heavy brunt of the water, listening to its chatter as it ran down the hill. I moved off the bridge, climbed some stairs cut into the hillside, and walked out of the tall trees that were lucky to have so much moisture close by. I headed up the trail, which started to switchback as it climbed, and I arrived breathing hard at a trail juncture. The trail sign nailed to a post said: THIS WAY TO THE HARDER ROUTE. That was the way for me.

The path started climbing through the trees for a good length of time, and then it came to a spot where they thinned out. Was this the top? No. I walked through it looking at the change in tree cover, wondering what had caused it. Less wind, more sun? The terrain here was a bit flatter but then it took off up the hill again. The trail wasn't in the trees so much anymore as the trees were trying to keep up with the trail. They lost. I traveled higher and walked on rocks, with the switchbacks coming quicker now. I had my wind now so going up didn't matter to me. I moved uphill briskly with the trail acting as more of a rock ladder in places. I wanted to see again from up here.

I got to a strong switchback up on the rock and could see a little trail off the main one that led onto the edge of the cliffs. I took it and saw the gorge spread before me. It was a stunning sight, like a Viewmaster scene, unreal, with things so far away yet perfectly real and clear. The tip of Mount Hood poked up over some hills over south on the Oregon side. The river from the dam wound its way past the cliffs toward the west and the ocean. It was easy to lose myself in these long vistas. I had to draw myself back in to remind myself where I was. Don't slip. Don't take too many chances climbing around these cliffs. Mistakes were deadly out here, even so close to civilization.

I thought about Wheaton, my old hiking companion. He had long ago left town to do his trekking and to work out some things for himself. He came back to the States after a few years and wrote a note to me every now and then. He ended up with a gal named Tootie who worked in the forest service in the Sierras down in California. They had some land next to the national forest and ran a pack service with goats for long trips into the mountains. Why should it make sense to me?

Still more uphill for me to climb. Which birthday hike up Mount Aaron was this one now? I thought of that first one so many years ago, when I was young. I had gone up it so fast on that clear day. I remembered another one done five or six years later on an April day when it was snowing. It's why I hiked on my birthday, to feel all the weather, to feel alive. To get drenched by the rain, hit by the hail. On the day it snows, it also clears up and the sun shines. It's every kind of weather coming up to greet me on that spring day and I felt alive being in it.

That one year, a friend of mine named Tony asked to come along on the hike. It was a cold rainy day for most of it. We got up as far as the saddle between the rock spire and the rest of the mountain that stretched back north. Up that high on the trail that day it was snowing, but the snow was coming in horizontally. It was fantastic weather. It wasn't sticking on the ground, so the path was obvious, but Tony got nervous. He was a more conservative kind of hiker. I couldn't believe it, but he thought we might get stuck up here and he didn't want to go up any higher. To my mind it was just getting good. The snow was blowing, we were warm and moving, and if we paid attention we would be fine on the trail. He would have none of it. We turned around and headed back downhill into the rain. It was better not to have him anxious on the walk. I thought to myself, These hikes are better when I'm alone. I can take the chances that I want and reap the rewards. Look at what we missed, a chance to get snowed on in the woods.

14

What We Can Agree Upon

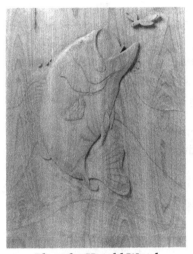

Photo by Harold Wood

There are only two things that wood-workers can agree upon.

Number one is that wood moves. It is alive. It seems so at least. Cut down a tree and soon after cutting it starts to check or crack at its end. If milled and put into the sun, it will start cracking all over the board. If one is careful to paint the ends of the log with a wax coating as soon as it's cut to slow down the drying, if one is thoughtful with the milling and dries the wood with care and time, sticks it out of the sun and the rain and provides air flow around it and lets it sit for a year or so per inch of thickness, you may find some beautiful lumber in those logs.

I can also buy lumber that has been kiln-dried, take it from its cozy home in the lumber rack and to my shop, and slice it in two, resawing it to reveal its elegant figure and grace. I can cut it for a beautiful book-matched figure and sometimes even then the wood moves. It can cup across its width like a bowl. Or bow along its length like the arc of the earth seen from above. There is such a moisture imbalance sometimes from the outside to the inside of the board that it moves like it never wants to be used. And so it shan't, as I have to toss it or use it to make wood bowties, like my friend Muggi in Iceland.

Wood moves. It responds to water. Some woods more than others. Some cuts cause more trouble than others. Flat-sawn or plain-sawn lumber cups more, especially over time, because the growth rings are bigger and wider at the sap-side face than the heart side. Wood moves. You can pay attention to this or ignore it, but woodworkers know that wood moves. I think wood is alive still and I always pay attention to grain direction and the way that wood will shrink. I used to fear getting my wood wet. I was always rushing home from the lumberyard before the rains or trying to tie my tarps down well enough, fearful of what that evil water would do to my wood.

One day I was at the lumberyard, and the clouds had darkened and it looked bad outside. I asked if they had some plastic to cover my load of lumber and plywood. They said yes, they could sell me some. I demurred on their kind offer and figured I would just hustle back to the shop and take my chances on the weather.

The weather laughed in my face. It chuckled. It guffawed. It spurted and laughed so hard it must have had rain coming out of its nose. Water poured down on me. It rained those great big drops that seem to be three raindrops all bunched together as one. It was a deluge, a flood, a wall of water coming down. I could barely see out the windshield of my truck. My pickup truck then was the one without the canopy. Yes that one, so I had nothing to protect my wood. There was my load of lumber and sheet goods soaking in all that liquid sunshine. I drove back to my shop, clouds inside the cab of the truck gathering over my forehead.

When I got there, most of the storm had ceased and was dripping off my lumber. I unloaded all the wood inside. I thought to myself, You know, I talk about lumber movement with my students all the time. In class, I take one of the studio's marketing pieces, a bookmark. A bookmark that is straight, made of heavy paper, and I hold it out and pour water on one face of it. It immediately bows and cups as the water is getting only one side wet. The paper soaks up the water and expands and moves. The other side, the dry side, gets pushed over. That's why wood warps. It is this imbalance between faces that is the issue, not the water.

The tree when standing is mostly water, and that's why a downed log is so heavy. Trees love water. Wood loves water. What's the worry about getting something wet if I can get the other side wet? I went to the sink and got a big towel soaking wet and wiped down the other faces of all my plywood and lumber. Everything stayed perfectly flat.

Wood moves.

ᔕ

The other thing—because remember I mentioned that there were two things we woodworkers could agree about—the other thing is very simple and probably knowledge as old and venerated as wood movement. It is likely carved in a calligraphic script in Latin onto a plaque hanging high in some forgotten British castle for all to see and marvel at:

Never mind those other woodworkers. They are ignorant, stubborn, and superstitious.

Everyone has their own method for just about everything in the shop. Everyone has a different way of sharpening their chisels or their scrapers. And everyone finishes differently or mills their lumber a certain special way. And if you hear of someone's approach or, God forbid, see it being done, you marvel to yourself at what a knucklehead this other craftsman is. How does he survive doing all these things so bass ackward? Lost all his good sense in the rain, has he?

~

I have a friend named Brian who is a marvelous designer and an exceptional engineer, and he has come into my studio several times to teach classes on chair making. Every class he would observe me as I helped him out with one job or another. I would perform an operation or two and while he wouldn't come right out and say that I was a cross-eyed village idiot, his manner did seem to suggest it. He was polite. He would stand quietly watching me, for example, drilling a hole in a board on the drill press. And he would just stand for a time and then he would ask me, "Is that the way you drill a hole?"

What? Of course. What had I just been doing? The response I wanted to make to him, because this wasn't the first or second time that he had commented on my ways, was: "Well hell no, that ain't the way I drill a hole. Usually I stand here naked drilling it except for my boots and my apron on of course, but I'm hiding my methods from you so you don't steal them because they're so superior to anything else you have ever seen . . . Of course it's the way I drill a hole. It's how I have always drilled a hole and it works. There, see. I have drilled a hole, now what's your problem?"

No, I would not say this.

I was polite. I would say, "Yes, this is how I drill a hole." Next he would go on to show me the error of my ways and his superiority, which he sometimes had, I'm not denying it, because he'd go and sharpen the drill bit a new way and adjust the speed and make a great clean cut and I'd go off mumbling and drill the same damn way I'd always drilled, next time out.

You just can't teach some people. Especially woodworkers.

BENCH MARK

This day was sunny on the trail up Mount Aaron. I walked along the ridge-line in the trees and then out again where you could see down into the valley to the northwest. A hawk came up the hillside from the treetops below me and passed close by, catching a spiral on the invisible wind. He left me below on the trail quickly. I kept walking and got a view where I could see off far to the west. Trees and hillsides, draining canyons, and there in the distance the Columbia, again moving off to the ocean. Big views. Lots of places to stop and contemplate my smallness.

I moved on. The altitude was making the firs and hemlocks grow smaller, work harder for life. I entered a dense grove of small firs, switchbacking quickly to keep up with the altitude gain, the creek running briefly down the center of the trail. Manzanita and vine maple worked for space. Then I was on the hillside, bare rock strewn with lichen. It was open to the sky, to the wind, and a few wildflowers had the courage to show their tiny faces to the sunshine. The vista was now south across the river to Oregon. The trail turned back into the brush again high over my head, back into shadow. I walked, but then saw just above me through the bush some boulders, and maybe the hint of bare ground or rock. There was a trail perhaps in the bushes, a bare spot of ground that went up into the brush.

I said, Why not. I dove into the bush and there it was, a faint trail, and it went toward the edge of the rock. I followed. It came out to the cliff edge, which was moss-covered, so it made it look benign, but I looked down and saw a short fall, then beyond that a hundred foot drop to rocks below. The birds alone could climb in this altitude. I moved away and uphill to a large boulder I found above me, scaled it, and sat down to take in the view. Surrounded by the viney bushes, it was a good sight to take in from up here.

Setting down my pack and reaching for my water bottle, I glanced at the rock underneath me, expecting to find moss and basalt, nothing more. There in the boulder was a surveyor's benchmark. A marker, a brass marker, a bit green in color and about 4" in diameter, that listed something in number and symbol for the Geodetic survey. I was too surprised by its placement to plumb its mystery.

Some surveyor had placed this marker way up here on this rock, buried it in the stone so that some other surveyor could place his staff or rod on it, or whatever surveyors did, and look across to the Oregon side or maybe back into the Washington wilderness and map out the area. What was it doing up here surrounded by spindly bushes and the sky? I sat for a time considering the oddity of finding this medallion in a rock on top of a hill in essentially the middle of nowhere. How many times had I walked past it and never been aware of its placement?

I tried to explore uphill from this rock but it was solid brush. I went back the way I came, back to the trail, and then up to the summit of Mount Aaron, which was surprisingly anticlimactic. From up here on a bald spot in the brush I got a good view of the mountain to the east. Sur Mountain. One of these days, I said to myself, I'll try that mountain. I turned around and headed back downhill. I couldn't believe my dumb luck that day to have found that marker. I still wasn't sure what it portended, maybe something about stumbling into something small and significant. Maybe it was simply a reminder to keep my eyes open.

15

The Psychic Network

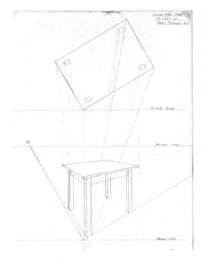

How many times have I had someone, a lawyer, a doctor, an engineer, come up to me at a show or in class and say to me, "I wish I had your life." The retort in my head of course was, "I wish I had your second house."

Nobody's life is perfect. As that philosopher Mr. Bob Dylan once wrote, "You're gonna have to serve somebody."

Why is it that people think that if they could become a full-time artist their life would change into a leisurely float down the river? Their life would be filled with Saturdays, that most blessed of days, when all there is to do is listen to the radio or plan a trip to the coffee shop. No obligations. It's just you and your wish list with no pressure. Great. Go down to the studio and put in some work time and just shut out the world and work. It'll be like that everyday if I finally give up this ridiculous job and its stress and its compromises on my life and turn, no, devote my life to my art. How much better life will be, now that I am a full-time artist?

All the working artists turn and grin to one another when they hear this. For this is the myth. Perhaps this is the very myth that drew each of them to this world. That it's just like a Saturday. Every day a Saturday without a boss bearing down on me. In truth, I have the worst and best kind of boss, myself. The one that knows how to push all my buttons, the one that is impatient, never satisfied with my performance, the one that always wants more from me. That one.

Unless they're also blessed with a business gene in them, most artists also stress about money and security for most of their working careers. Yes, they get to do the work at which they are gifted, but that sense of financial collapse is always at the back of their minds. Artists don't come to their work from a business perspective. You know the old joke: How do you make a million dollars building furniture? Start with two.

When I started I thought what I needed was to build a roomful of furniture and there would be my showroom and away I would go. Word would get out and the work would find me. I also became a woodworker because I didn't want a job marketing and selling. I would wake up in the morning and ask myself: What am I going to do today? This was a great feeling because there was no clock to punch, no boss to placate, I didn't have to rush in and be on time and get a box full of parts made. This was easy. I was going to build something today, somehow.

And then the end of the month would come around with its reality check.

I would be working on a challenging piece and I would be learning new techniques, trying out new ideas that were great for my education and terrible for my bottom line. I would look up and see the calendar and my rent checks were due, which I could cover. But what about after that? What would happen then?

Believe me when I say this, for it's true.

I would contact the psychic network.

I'm not suggesting that I called a TV hotline to ask a psychic where my future might lie. But there was this weird thing that always occurred when I needed work and I started to think about it. Work would show up. I'd get to my desk and start calling up folks I knew to see if they needed something made, or maybe they had a friend who needed something made. And the answer was usually no. Then a week later, two weeks later, someone else would call up and ask me to do a job. It was as if the universe was listening in on my phone calls, took pity on me, and threw me another bone to let me continue on. It was kind or cruel enough to throw me a scrap but no more than that, just enough money to keep me at the bench, to make me think, Hey, maybe I can make this work. And that was okay.

The incredible thing was that this approach worked at all. I found that by putting out good energy to the world it bounced some back to me. This was a simple concept. Luck is being prepared for the time when the world throws something back at me. After that the rest is up to me. When the studio hit the hard times that everyone except the bankers had during the recession I would tell my assistants, we have to be positive. We have to put out good energy and good energy will come back to us. I do not know how this happens. I do not subscribe to any theory or religion or organized group that believes in this spiritual stuff. I only know that energy rebounds. Get out there and start talking to people and something good will come from it. Maybe it's those weak ties to people that Malcolm Gladwell refers to in *The Tipping Point*. Or maybe it is simply the universe hearing our prayer.

I might point out to the god that took and answered my messages that she could have sent me bigger jobs than what she did, but I'm not complaining. There were always jobs and as long as I kept working and didn't want for too very much, I could keep my complaining down and the happiness of coming to the bench alive.

If I wanted to live a life where I created things, then certain consequences occurred for me. I didn't marry or inherit well, so I was not going to be rich. I would not get to take expensive vacations or jet to the coast to party on the weekends. The poverty train instead had a seat marked out just for me. I had to learn to get by and be smart and not profligate with my resources, making do with less because there were other rewards that came with my work. I needed to stay focused and on task, always steering toward my goal. Even when I got blown off course, even when I fell asleep and drifted, I always had to come back to my path in order to reap those rewards.

A friend and colleague once asked me how I had the courage to make that choice for myself. Well, it was easy. I didn't want to do what was expected of me. I wanted to make up my own path. There were of course great names ahead of me to aspire to: Wharton Esherick, George Nakashima, Art Espenet Carpenter. I took it upon myself to learn what I could in my own way and see what kind of mess I could make of it. It takes a belief in yourself and a commitment to doing your best work and believing that somehow it will be found.

I would still get upset sometimes at how little money I was making to produce work at such a high level. I finally got fed up with my own complaining. I said to myself one day, "I don't get paid for this perfection. If I choose to do this nitpicky, crazy obsessive stuff I will not be paid for it. So do it and shut up. Or don't do it, drop my standards, and move on. Don't think about my poverty. I chose this. Live with it."

It helped me to be calmer with myself.

Doing this work takes a degree of selfishness too. I have to be good at it for reasons almost unspecifiable to others because it matters more to me than anything else. So every day I must practice. Why not work on

Sundays? It's my hobby, it's my play, it's my life. It doesn't take courage to do this. It takes fear, in a strange and curious way. I cannot fail to do this work. If I do fail at doing it, at making the time, or by picking an easier path, I will let myself down in a way that will be too much to bear. I must do the work.

⌒

If every day isn't a Saturday and there are money issues, how do you manage the stress of that? Poverty wears on you. It takes over your days and your nights. It took some years to get to a place to understand that money is not evil and it is not good. It is not bad to have it and not bad to spend it. What I saw money mostly do for others was to buy them stuff without making them happy. So I understood that having money doesn't bring happiness. It eliminates an unhappiness, which is poverty. This seems obvious but it took me time to get this straight in my head. When I did, it was easier to stay on my path.

I once gave a lecture to some community college students about craft. These were people involved in boatbuilding, cabinetry, and carpentry. My talk was about design, doing good work, and quality. One student raised her hand and asked, "How are we supposed to do this today? No one's buying work so how can we put extra effort in doing quality when no one wants to pay for it? They want really good work but for IKEA prices."

I told them this life is not for everyone. It's a tough way to earn a buck. The same could be said of farming or throwing pots or being a chef. It is a choice that once made places you swimming upstream against our consumer culture. It is a strong current that flows against thinking for oneself, that pushes against the value of quality, that trumpets the virtues of the crowd and the trend over the individual. This is a culture that wants to ship out work by hand overseas or to the newest and lowest-paid immigrants. One that considers doing work with our hands beneath our standards of dignity. Becoming an artist in today's world is a choice that still needs an explanation for most people. Even some of our best known artists don't find value in process and in using their hands. Let a computer paint my painting or lay down a drum track or cut up my wood.

Why become a poet? We don't need them. Why study the violin? It's a hard life. Why learn how to build fine furniture? Who can afford this preciousness? It's work, but it is not remunerative in any way when you're young. You starve, you have to scrape by, you have to sacrifice as you learn ways to market your work, make yourself known, and develop a reputation. Maybe after twenty-five years you will be discovered.

As long as you satisfy that urge in you to be creative, if you keep that spirit of curiosity alive and always strive to make your work better, what more do you need out of life? You have found a purpose. The universe will provide for you in some fashion.

This is what I know. Woodworking is a tough way to make a living. It's a great way to live.

Every day isn't a Saturday. It's a Tuesday morning that's partly cloudy with a 30 percent chance of rain and the saw is out of alignment. There's work to be done. And if you made the right choice for your temperament and style, it will make sense for you to be there. Even on those days when you're cranky, when you don't want to work hard, and you don't make much money doing it, if it's right, then you will feel good doing this work. One day, you may be able to look back and say to yourself, "That was a good choice."

Get busy.

⟿

Letter from a student in June 2004:

> Dear Gary, I was wondering if you could lend some general advice. I want to start a career in woodworking, cabinetry specifically. This will be a career shift for me. Though I do have woodworking and tool/equipment experience, I have no portfolio. How do apprenticeships stack up against a course (like yours or at Seattle College) as a way to get into the field? I'm a bit older than most people entering the apprenticeship, 32, and thought that a specialized course would be a better alternative for me. Now I wonder, will this over qualify me for many positions? G.

> Hi G.,

> If you apprentice at a cabinet shop you will learn how to make cabinets. If you study at a fine woodworking school, you will learn how to build fine furniture. The first will pay your bills and bore you to tears. The second will almost pay your bills and keep your step lively for years. We are always faced with these damned choices. Sincerely, Gary

PACIFIC HEIGHTS LIBRARY

I was in San Francisco visiting a friend. She had an apartment on one side of Pacific Heights, that ridge that overlooks the bay and the Golden Gate Bridge. So when she was at work, I thought I'd explore the area. It was a lovely sunny day and I was strolling the streets and drinking in the city.

It's an uphill walk to the Heights from anywhere, but the scenery was nice and the architecture of the houses started to intrigue me. I always carried a notebook with me filled with unlined paper to draw out ideas. As I walked I sketched designs or details that I saw on buildings or homes. I was right up on top of the Heights, walking down the street, when I was struck by a detail on a Georgian-style box of a house. Something about the columns surrounding the front door and a detail at the roofline made me stop to sketch them out. At the edge of the lawn, expansive for a San Francisco home, a man was talking with a gardener. I thought they were at the house next door. As the man turned and walked toward me I realized that no, I was standing in front of this gentleman's house.

He was a man in his seventies, perhaps. He was cordial. He was polite. He asked me, "What are you doing?"

I told him, "I'm a furniture maker and I'm sketching ideas for pieces. Is this your house? I'm just sketching some details I liked."

"Yes, it is my house. Oh, you like furniture do you?" he asked.

"Well, yes, it's what I do, I design and build furniture, custom furniture."

"Oh, what kind?"

"Wood furniture," I replied, "sort of an modern Asian Arts and Crafts style." This of course only narrowed the selection to about four thousand years of furniture design. "It's a mix," I modified.

"Well," he said, "I have some furniture you might like to see."

The untrusting part inside me turned invisibly and looked around for a camera on us or a witnesses in case I was about to be killed. It was an odd sort of invitation I thought from a complete stranger based on my poor standing sketch of his San Franciscan manse, but it was an invitation nevertheless. I said, "I'd love to."

We walked up the perfect straight Georgian sidewalk to his front door. Columns framed the doorway and gave it a bit of an imposing entry. Nothing too grand, it was a restrained home painted in white, the roof in black. As we got up to the door he started talking again. "You know I don't just let people into my house."

I couldn't have agreed more with him. "I understand completely." I was hoping he didn't have bodies buried in the basement. My look at the time was not too disheveled and I was sketching so he could see that I wasn't lying about that. I assumed that I looked like a safe bet to him, but who knew about this rich guy?

Then he said, "You know, my wife is in the hospital." Oh boy, I thought, this is it. Poor old guy, I thought to myself. He's one of those lonely old fellows who's dying to talk with someone because he feels so all alone and helpless, and I fell right into the trap. He will invite me in and tell me his life story and it will take up the rest of my afternoon. Oh well, I let myself in for this.

"She's got cancer. She's down at Stanford."

"I'm sorry to hear it."

"I'm head of surgery there." Whoa. I didn't say that but I thought it. Whoa on two counts.

He opened the door to a nondescript and dark hallway. The feel of the rooms was classic. They were smallish but with no imagination in their layout. The house was a box cut up into smaller boxes. He showed me a small table by the doorway, an Ethan Allen piece at best, brown-red stain on neoclassical lines. It was a simple piece. He took me next to the small study by the front of the house. Here he started to tell me about this desk that had one door falling off its hinges. It was nothing to brag about so I didn't congratulate him. I was polite and practiced my mumble for him. Next he showed me a painting or two, portraits conveying neither great style nor great emotion. I stayed polite and took the tour with him.

We walked past the kitchen to the small dining room in back. There were windows on both sides of the room so it had some light. A small door was placed at the back of the room directly across from where we had entered. A servants' door? The room was filled with the dining table, dark brown, as were the sideboard and serving table. All dark brown, nicer than the other furniture in the house but no better than top-of-the-line manufactured work. I admired the furniture as best I could but it was still a stretch. I was deep into the house by now and would have needed a giant crow bar to pry myself from this situation. I would have to ride this out and hope it helped him somehow to give me this tour, to assuage his loneliness.

Then, after a time that I shared with him unknowing, a time of weighing, a time of consideration, a time of decision, he finally said to me, "Well, if you like furniture, come look at this." And he opened the narrow door at the rear of the dining room. I walked in and found myself standing on a small landing. Below me was a room as big as a small library. Which it was. Two stories tall within, it was all brown wood, all French oak, all from a castle in France, he told me. My mouth opened and hung there. He had bought the library in France and had it transported here and stuck onto the back of his house. My mouth still obeyed gravity. Through tall windows at the back of the room one could see out to the bay and the Golden Gate Bridge. It was a stunning view. *I* was stunned. He had been testing me, all along the way, testing me to see if I was trustworthy, testing me to see if I would be suitably impressed. I'm not sure what he was testing me for. Did he need to hear me gasp at his fortune? At his life? I am not sure even to this day, but gasp I did. I almost fell to my knees in astonishment. The woodwork, the vista, the size of the room, all these things behind a simple austere Georgian house.

He gave me a tour of the library. He showed me the flooring, the walls, the dovetail-inlaid keys in the French oak wood panels, and the doorway to the secret passage under the house, although he didn't take me through there. It's just as well, I was too stunned with disbelief to take in much more. I couldn't believe what I had been shown. I asked him if I could take a photograph or two. He agreed, seeing that I had become a tourist. I took a few dim photographs and that was it. I was led back to the front of the house and shown the door. "Have a pleasant day," he offered and then I was set free. Released.

To what? What had just happened? My patience had been tried and tested and I was rewarded for I know not what purpose. I thanked the fates and hoped his wife would get better, and I went on with my walk. Suffice it to say that I did not see anything else that day comparable to that library.

Patience, dear boy, I told myself, patience. I had learned that day that discovery is sometimes about patience. It is about waiting. One never knows if one's patience will be met with kindness or reward or with absolutely nothing. And sometimes you must just wait. My own patience was given a gift that sunny day.

Patience is also a form of action.
—Auguste Rodin, sculptor

16

Ruby's Knees

Photo by Jim Piper

Most people associate woodworking with sanding. It is inevitable because everyone loves to feel smooth wood, to run their hands over an exquisite surface. How many folks have touched my work and moaned, "I love how smooth this feels." Of course, it's wood. It's smooth, warm, and sensual, no doubt of that.

How do you make wood smooth? For most folks it means sanding. It means learning the fascinating difference between garnet sandpaper, good for hand sanding, and aluminum oxide, good for power sanding. And what is this wet/dry silicon carbide paper that is so dark-looking? Why is this sandpaper so good but so expensive? It's because it stays sharper and is glued down with a waterproof glue. You can use it wet or dry, with water or with an oil. Versatile stuff.

Then there are grits. Grit refers not to a food item or the quality of someone's character. It does not suggest that this person has sand between their teeth. It does refer to the size of the sanding particles glued to the paper. So a very coarse grit, one used for sanding rough floors, is 36 grit. A fine grit is 400 grit, which is used for polishing a board or to apply an oil finish. I use 2000 grit for the final smoothing of a finish, and it feels like glass when you're done sanding with that smooth a paper.

As a woodworker, I learned to sand carefully, working my way up through the grits from coarse to fine. First I remove the milling marks left behind by the jointer or planer. These are not design features in the wood. Get rid of those. Then I move on to smoothing the surface with a finer paper, being careful not to leave sanding swirls behind from the sander and remembering to sand *with* the grain, not cross grain, because otherwise this will reveal the end grain fibers, which are more porous. If I sand or scratch them open, they will absorb more finish and look darker than I intend. My poor sanding technique then becomes more apparent. Be careful. Three or four sandings like this over the entire surface of a project becomes a bunch of work. It's time consuming. Finally and above all, it's boring as hell.

While sanding, just how many times can you relive your high school triumphs? I can recall the only time I did something right on the baseball field for my father, the coach. So that goes by pretty fast. But how many times the failures? How many times could I remember the loves in my life? My sweetie Donna in junior high bringing me cookies at basketball practice is a fond memory, but hardly worthy of a long stretch of daydreaming. I had days of sanding time ahead of me on projects. This wasn't a task. It was a labor. This wasn't some easy job like Hercules mucking out the stables. This was sanding. And, because it made me look so carefully at my work looking for scratches, I became obsessed with perfection.

I needed good light to see my work, or rather my poor work, where I had scratches remaining and where I needed to sand more and where I missed a spot. I kept missing spots! I kept working surfaces, sanding over and over, because sanding wants you to make everything perfect. It forces you into this place where you are trying to be perfect and it's maddening. Because you know what perfect feels and looks like. If your standards are set high like mine were, it is . . . very . . . time . . . consuming. I wore through my finger tips sanding. They would become red with the effort. I bled on my work. I went out and bought office worker's rubber finger tips to protect my fingers.

Sanding made me more obsessive, striving for perfection, setting impossible standards for smoothness, and it wore me out. What's not to love about it?

⮌

One day I was working on a design for a coffee table with great shapely legs. It had a classical shape like a cabriole leg, yet it wasn't a Chippendale eighteenth-century design. It was more classical, like a Chinese table, but it wasn't quite that either. It was a synthesis of styles that I had come up with quite by accident, like all good design. When it came to me, I worked and worked it until it grew off the pages of my notebooks and into reality. I had first built this table as a model, spending three hours, like my brief mentor Art Carpenter had showed me, making this model true to life in detail and color and wood. It was magical enough that I had my photographer at the time take a photo of it so I could convince a gallery to take the piece. Which they did. The model was that good. I liked the piece and I started to make this table for clients.

The table I called Ruby's Knees. Ruby was the pseudonym of the crazy lady whose house I was renting a room in at the time. Crazy not because she was madly in love with her girlfriend Trisha the actress, blonde and gorgeous. Who wouldn't walk around drunk with love for her? No, and not crazy because she worked at a restaurant till 1 a.m. or so and then came home to host poker games and do drugs with her friends till dawn. No, she was crazy because she was crazy. And Ruby was her crazy name that she gave herself, and so these legs I designed with her name because they looked nothing like her although they sort of looked like someone's legs. There's design logic for you.

I was done building the table and had started to apply my finish. I was in my old shop at the warehouse down in the gully. My work was done for the day. I had put on my second coat on Ruby's tabletop with an oil/varnish mixture and I wiped it dry. I made sure that I spread out all my rags to dry, and I walked to the door, shut off the lights to my shop, and turned to look back at my work for the day. It's satisfying to savor these moments. The northern light coming through the wall of windows was just enough to see my shop there in shadow, and I looked out these windows and back to my world that I had created and to the table I had built. It made quite a picture. The shop in the dim light, the tools there in their stately silence, all the benches and cabinets, the lumber racks and the table.

The table, regal, classical, quiet and glowing with . . .

[Imagine my voice quiet at first in disbelief.] "What the hell is that?" I stared at the tabletop.

[Imagine my voice a bit louder now querying.] "What the hell is on the top?"

[Imagine my voice loud now with astonishment.] "What is that line, that stripe running across my table? What the hell is that?"

I walked up to the table and looked at it in disbelief. I had sanded this table to within an inch of its life and mine. I had first taken it to get it surfaced at a friend's shop because he had what is called a wide-belt sander. He had sanded it perfectly flat, and then I had sanded it and raised the grain with water and sanded it again and again and once more for good measure. I had run my hand repeatedly across its smooth surface.

What was that line? I demanded.

I got down on my knees to look. The sanding machine had left a line of snipe in it. A line where the board had leapt into the sanding drum just at the last two inches or so of the board. Nothing you could feel. Nothing you could see. But with two coats of finish on it, with the light just right coming across the room, that good northern light, even and consistent, that light bounced off the tabletop right up to my eyes and there it was. Plain as a stripe across the road.

Snipe. On my Ruby's Knees.

My crest was fallen. I was, if not crushed, at least severely disappointed, because it meant only one thing. I would have to start over. I would have to scrape off the finish. I would have to start my sanding all over again because I could not have a sanding snipe across this beautiful tabletop. I could not have it. I had to sand it all over again.

I learned many things from that snipe in Ruby's tabletop: that sanding can make me go crazy, that perfection can be evil and not good, and that the combination of the two can numb the mind. I had hoped everything was right when it wasn't. I also learned to hand plane and scrape because that way I eliminate milling marks and snipe and it's actually faster smoothing up. Wetting down large surfaces with a solvent to check them for scratches or things I missed also works wonders. Finally I learned, once more, to slow down.

> Finally I learned once more to slow down.

SUR MOUNTAIN

I had been staring at Sur Mountain for a long time now. Every drive down the gorge I would look across the river at it. And every trip I took up Mount Aaron, when I would get to the top and stare off east toward Mount Adams, that beast of a volcano another hour away, I would see Sur Mountain there in front of my eyes. I kept saying to myself that one of these days I would tackle it.

It was on one of my birthday hikes in April that the beagle and I tried it finally. We started among the power lines down low near Bonneville Dam and walked in and among clear cuts and tick country for a time, picking up the Pacific Crest Trail. The walking was easy but the trail snaked back and forth through the clear cuts like somebody had been drinking the day they laid this path out.

We crossed the logging access road and came to that first lake close by the power lines and we hiked past that to another smaller lake. Off in the distance we could hear gunfire that I hoped was moving away from us. I thought maybe it was a shooting range, the best possible scenario I could come up with. We hiked for another three or four hours in mostly flat land surrounded by the forest. It was fine enough in the dappled sunlight that day. The beagle and I stopped for a snooze at some campsite near a creek and then kept on toward that mountain, our goal.

We arrived finally at what could only be called the stairway up. It was a ridgeline that we followed straight up the mountain and it was tough going for the beagle and me. We made it up to timberline after an hour or so and still had another chunk of footage to climb to get to the top of the mountain. We sat for lunch instead. Where we perched seemed as high as Mount Aaron ever got. It was so close, almost touchable to the southwest of us. We were on the edge of the world on this thin ridgeline. Nothing but sky and hilltops to see. We still had more to go to get to the top. It was a magnificent view but the wind was blowing hard uphill and the slope was slippery. It was a worthy hike even not making the top. We had done good. I congratulated us.

I had my socks off to dry them and to cool my toes and out of nowhere this hiker, the only other guy we'd seen all day, just walked by us up the ridge. He was as surprised to see us sitting there as we were to see him. He waved and kept heading up the mountain. The beagle and I had done enough up for that day. Looking up at the top of Sur Mountain, it was a long pull to finish it up. I turned us around to make the long return trip home. I about ruined my feet on that walk. I wore slippers to work for a month after that with the pain as a reminder of that day. It was worth it. Long hikes don't take on their real value until you savor them in memory.

17

The Center of the Universe

Photo by Harold Wood

I am a peripatetic woodworker. I move from one project to another, always looking to find something new to arouse my curiosity. The same is true for my teaching method. I go from one idea to another in my lectures. I land on one subject like flatness as a concept and then bounce off to talking about winding sticks and sawhorses and my bench and how valuable they are to my work. I have an outline of topics always at my side that I can just pay attention to because there is so much information out there, so much to show people. There are so many cool things to discuss and pull together and engage folks in the idea of how the world is indeed an incredibly small place in all its vastness. This particular truth came to me during a lecture on precision.

⟳

Stick with this fact: your workbench is the center of the universe.

Not everyone will get this concept right off. Some might even resist, so fill this in for people.

Your workbench is where everything gets built. It has to be sturdy and outfitted with a strong vise. It has to be flat, heavy, and solid. When you pound on it, your bench needs to handle it. It has to be too heavy to lift by yourself. It has to be the maypole around which your work dances every day.

Now saying that my bench is the center of the universe may seem a bit defensive to some. To others it may appear to be an unsubstantiated, even wildly off-kilter claim made by an insecure, myopic, or perhaps drunken craftsman. Yet I know that it's true. I learned to build work on my bench with this kind of confidence.

Why is this necessary? Because someday a client will call and say to you, "We moved that really precious piece you built to the other side of the room. The door won't shut now." Or, "Why do we need that shim under the table leg?" Or, "How come the drawer sticks?" Your reply is always the same: "My bench is the center of the universe. When I built it here, it was perfect." (Be firm in voice when you say this.)

It really is quite simple. When I build on a true, flat, and untwisted surface, then my work has a better chance of being built right. When I glue up boards for a tabletop for instance, my bench is flat, the clamp bars are flat, the lumber is milled flat. Any one of those things can cause problems with a glue-up so I eliminate them. The work can then be defended with impunity, with surety, with confidence.

Know too that houses, old and new, have uneven floors or walls that aren't plumb. They sag and floors can twist over time. You should expect this. I have a tall cabinet that I made and put into my ninety-year-old house. The cabinet door will open perfectly if it sits to the right of the front door. Moved to the left side of the entryway, the door barely opens and once open it is a struggle to shut completely. I have to shim it a quarter inch at the rear leg to account for the unevenness of the floor. Gravity, like rust, never sleeps. So if you load up a cabinet or bookcase with stuff, since they have no bracing across their front face, your doors will twist or won't open or close properly. It's no grand mystery to solve.

Tell your clients this: Here on my bench, the piece was perfect. It was flat. The door swung sweetly, the drawer slid smoothly. Here, on my bench, I made it just right. Then it went to your twisted, cracked, and possessed house and everything changed. Here at my bench, I built it right, and now it's different. Blame gravity, not me. At the center of the universe that piece was fine.

Do your best work always and you can defend it every time. Then offer them a shim for the leg. Stuff happens. Mention that too.

Backside Trail

The beagle and I went up Mount Aaron a few times together. He was never impressed by the views, but he loved the smells on the trail. One time we were up on the summit surrounded by scrub brush. This little bald spot at the back of the mountain's head has no place to sit or take in the view. I could just see the top of Mount Hood and the river view was mostly blocked up there, so we walked on the trail north away from home. We found some rocks where I could sit and take in the view of Sur Mountain, and I spread out lunch. The beagle joined me of course. Even good smells didn't trump food to his way of thinking.

Looking at Sur Mountain, it's clear that half of it slumped off. It has such a dramatic loss of its south side. The lichenometrists and dendrochronologists may try to pinpoint the geological dates of this landslide by studying fungi and tree rings, but the Native legends make better sense of things.

⤚

Two brothers, Klickitat and Wy'east, traveled with their father, the chief of all the gods, Tyhee Saghalie, to the Columbia River, looking for a place to live. They found a spot near the Dalles that was so beautiful that both sons wanted it. They quarreled over it and the father settled the argument by shooting one arrow north of the river and one arrow south. Klickitat went north and lived there and Wy'east moved south. The chief then built a bridge over the river, Bridge of the Gods, to connect the two so they could meet.

The sons then both fell in love with the maiden Loowit, but she could not choose between them. They fought over her, destroying the land, villages, forests. The bridge fell into the river, creating the rapids. Tyhee Saghalie punished them all by turning them into mountains. One son, Wy'East, became the proud mountain known to the whites as Hood. The other was turned into Mount Adams, which looked back to where Loowit had been turned into the fire mountain to the west, St. Helens.

⤚

My sight and thoughts went out into the distance. I looked again at Sur, the partially collapsed mountain closest to us. What was left of the mountain was flat on top. It was a long pull to get only halfway up that thing, I remembered. I thought back to having lunch there, sitting on the rocks in the sunshine. I congratulated myself that on this walk today I had on some good boots.

I finished up and, as the beagle and I had never seen where the trail went when it headed north up here on Mount Aaron, I thought what the heck, we can't get too lost. And if we do get lost or don't like where we're walking we can turn around and come back the way we came. We headed off down the back ridge of the mountain.

What is it about me that gets so comfortable with a routine, a menu, a route to work, a way of doing things that no other way is even admissible as evidence? Impossible, my brain says. There's only *this* good way. Well, this back trail was proving me wrong, again. For years I went down Mount Aaron the way I came up, the hard way, the steep way, the precipitous way. There was another way down. I realized as we walked that this was the easy route I had never wanted to walk. This trail was open to the sky and I could see that we were now circling back west around the peak and down into a valley.

We found not just trail but roads up near the top. I suspected they mined or logged up here for a time. A path took us north, downhill away from my truck. The beagle and I went down it for a time but I didn't want to have to come back a long way up this trail. It was a sunny and pleasant day so why not sit in the shade of the trees and have some lunch and a snooze? The beagle watched over me.

After our nap we turned and headed back uphill and followed the logging road south down into the trees. It was easy walking and it took us to a creek that drained the valley we were in. This was the valley the lazy hawk rose out of on his currents. The trees weren't too large here, some big-leaf maples mixed in, and the creek was fine and chuckling along at its own pace. There were even some picnic tables. This was a route I had never ever considered. I didn't even know it existed yet here we were.

I kept smacking myself figuratively upside the head as I walked down the trail. "See, there are other ways," I said to myself. There always are. Discovery of something so plain, so obvious, made me shake my head. I have to keep learning these lessons it seems. There are other points of view, other ways of solving problems. I had to quit believing that there was only one right way home.

18

The Oak Beams of New College, Oxford

GREGORY BATESON, 1982,
CO-EVOLUTION QUARTERLY

[There is debate about some of Bateson's facts in this quotation. I include this piece as an incentive to thought, not as historical fact. Gregory Bateson was an English anthropologist, social scientist, and philosopher. This story illustrates how consideration for the future can shape our decision-making today. My friend Ed gave me this quotation printed onto a T-shirt as a source of inspiration, or perhaps as a nod from a kindred spirit.]

"New College, Oxford, is of rather late foundation, hence the name. It was probably founded around the late sixteenth-century. It has, like other colleges, a great dining hall with big oak beams across the top, yes? These might be eighteen inches square, twenty feet long.

"Some five to ten years ago, so I am told, some busy entomologist went up into the roof of the dining hall with a penknife and poked at the beams and found that they were full of beetles. This was reported to the college council, who met in some dismay, because where would they get beams of that caliber nowadays?

"One of the Junior Fellows stuck his neck out and suggested that there might be on College lands some oak. These colleges are endowed with pieces of land scattered across the country. So they called in the College Forester, who of course had not been near the college itself for some years, and asked him about oaks.

"And he pulled his forelock and said, 'Well sirs, we was wonderin' when you'd be askin.'

"Upon further inquiry it was discovered that when the College was founded, a grove of oaks had been planted to replace the beams in the dining hall when they became beetly, because oak beams always become beetly in the end. This plan had been passed down from one Forester to the next for four hundred years. 'You don't cut them oaks. Them's for the College Hall.'

"A nice story. That's the way to run a culture."

⌒

Do your work as if no one will ever notice it but as if the world depends upon it.

DAMN RIGHT

To get good at something requires a great deal of practice. It might take a lifetime to master something. It can be hard to keep your head up. It is so worth the effort if you have the staying power, if you can continue to believe in yourself.

This is a prayer for when things get hard on your journey. This prayer needs to be read whenever you need it. Repeat it out loud, very loud. Pronounce it in private in your studio or say it to yourself while walking in the woods. Recite it alone on the beach screaming into the wind. Practice it on the subway, which is a surefire way to get yourself plenty of space for your ride home. Repeat the refrain after each lament.

> *Damn Right* (a prayer)
> Nobody knows how hard this work is.
>   Damn Right.
> I'm a great fool to make this my life.
>   Damn Right.
> And nobody knows how lonely I feel.
>   Damn Right.
> Or sees I can't take much more of this deal.
>   Damn Right.
> Nobody knows how good quitting would seem.
>   Damn Right.
> Let go of the struggle, slip into the stream.
>   Damn Right.

Nobody's glass is as half-empty as mine.
    Damn Right.
Everyone else has this dialed in just fine.
    Damn Right.
But no one can say this exactly like me.
    Damn Right.
The world hasn't seen what I bring to this scene.
    Damn Right.
I want the chance to shine and get my time.
    Damn Right.
My voice should be heard, my visions, design.
    Damn Right.
My work has value, my ideas have truth.
    Damn Right.
My voice is gold, it needs to be heard.
    Damn Right.
It's my time to shine, to shout out my words.
    Damn Right.
Wake up, world, I'm coming.
    Damn Right.

ACT THREE:

FORGIVENESS AND MASTERY

19

The Problem at the Bench

Photo by Harold Wood

The problem at the bench is always me. I forget why I am there in the first place. It is not to be building things, although that is grand. It is not to be learning a skill, which is also a great blessing. It is not to become familiar with a rich tradition of making, a broad history of craftsmanship that stretches back for centuries, to be part of a long progression of design and technical achievements. These are all very good, but none of these are the main reason why I am there.

I am there at the bench to be quiet with myself.

I was walking the beagle in my neighborhood one morning and I heard someone practicing violin in their house as we passed by. The player wasn't new at it, but neither was he skilled. He was learning and repeating his scales. Even I knew it wasn't a beginner's set as there were some small variations in them each time he played. He was halting at times, but on he pressed.

The violin scales ebbed in volume as we walked away down the sidewalk. I realized that in the hands of a great player these scales would have had a precision to them that this relative beginner lacked. They would have had a sound that was different, an intimate familiarity that would have made each note separate, rich, and clear. Even though both players would have played the same notes, the pupil would make his into mere sound while the master would have made hers brilliant. Yet it was inspiring to hear the pupil trying, practicing.

⌒

Everyone starts at the beginning.

When we are beginning, we are driftless. It's a difficult place to be. We become anxious because we don't have a direction picked out, a spot on which to stand to let our worth shine through. We're lost but we blame the world for not revealing itself to us. We shout, "Show me what I should be doing and I'll do It. I just don't know what that It is. I'm ready for It. I'll be great at It, once It shows up. All I need is a spot and then I'll shine like no one else ever has."

Our expectations of ourselves, our dreams and hopes of being great, our impatience gets in the way of our quest. Our standards come in so impossibly high that there is no way a beginner can meet them. A beginner knows what great looks like and know his own work is certainly not great at first. Frustration sets in. It's easier to quit and try something else than to continue on in this poor fashion. "Look at this terrible work, look at me, I failed again." Quitting is the simple way out. And the circle goes round and round.

I remember when I first started. I was raw. I had no talents, and no idea of whether they were deeply hidden or simply not there at all. It is terrifying to make a choice to do something and then be so inept at it. I would get angry with myself for making so many mistakes, one more stupid than the last. It was not pretty. Simple things, things I should remember and pay attention to, I would forget again and again. I knew what I wanted my work to be. And I wanted it now, not later. It was not easy to be bad at something that I desired so much.

Patience was never my strong suit. When I hiked, I wanted to be first up the mountain. When I ran I wanted to win. When I did anything, I was competing. I was in a hurry. Perhaps the speed at which I led my life was some indication of how much I wanted to run from things: my tough father, my own ridiculous and impossible self-imposed standards of perfection, my lack of trust in people, or perhaps my conviction that people were out for themselves. At the bench, I am competing with only myself, so why not lighten up? I was angry with myself much of the time when I was learning because I was never perfect. It was a contest that I could never win.

Know this as well: a perfectionist like myself never congratulates himself for getting close. When I made any mistake I was failing—and that was bad. Failure is a familiar cloak to wear. I could castigate myself with volume for any flaw in my work because it was so easy to be that way. I was only as good as myself, which was never good enough.

The task of learning can seem gigantic to the beginner. As an artist, you have to learn how to use the tools and materials, discover how things go together, and then there's design. It's a big mountain of experience to climb. You can forget that in the middle of all this is *you*. That great mass of inadequacies, complete with your desires, your expectations in the face of your failures, and your lack of patience or your lack of humor. You're in the way of things, impatient to be great. "I can flip the switch of a tool. Why can't I flip a switch and just be great?"

The truth is that one of the hardest things I had to learn is how to fail. Henry Petroski is an author and professor of civil engineering at Duke University.

Failure is how we learn. We acknowledge our ignorance first and ask for help. We try to correct it.

One of the overarching concerns in his books is the importance of failure and its importance in how we design and how we learn. Read his wonderful book, *The Evolution of Useful Things*. Inventors design things because they are driven by the perceived failure of a current design. Is a function being properly performed or can it be improved? Petroski understands the necessity of failure in order to push an idea forward, whether it be on an engineering problem or one of technique or design. He quotes Thomas Edison: "Genius. Sticking to it is the genius . . . I failed my way to success."

Failure in design is as important as failure in construction. As one of Petroski's chapter titles points out, form follows failure. Form doesn't follow function. Failure is the means by which we all learn to do better.

The importance of failure has been lost in most of our educational system. It has a pejorative meaning, as if it's something to be eradicated. As Mark, a botanist friend of mine who studies seeds for the USDA, told me: "If the error is consistent for a scientist, then you have proved something. This is valuable. If the results are consistent with your presumption of error, then the experiment that fails is a success."

People today fear the idea of failing. They become virtual players rather than active participants, choosing to watch video rather than try and fail themselves at something. They fear looking ignorant. I tell my students not to fear their ignorance; ignorance is curable. It's stupidity I can do nothing with. Failure is how we learn. We acknowledge our ignorance first and ask for help. We try to correct it. It's a risk. At the bench, I try my hands on the tool one way and make a cut. It doesn't feel right. That's okay. Move my hands and try them in a new position. If this grip works, it will become a part of my language at the bench. This takes time. The issue is whether we can handle this correction of our ignorance with humility and patience or whether our frustrations will limit us. Persisting through failure deserves the medal, not simple participation. Fail in order to succeed better.

⌒

In class one day, I had an engineer who worked on Nike's Manufacturing Innovation Team, figuring out how they would make shoes ten years from now. He told me that a shoe has two hundred or so touch points, when someone touches the shoe during the manufacturing process. He was making a spoon that day in class and said, "I've already had about one thousand touch points on this spoon today." He was learning about which touch points were right or better and which were wrong. In his world, he would have determined which of those touch points he could eliminate to cut costs and save resources. In mine, I decide which ones to keep that yield better, more beautiful results.

As we lose our hands-on classes in schools, we lose failure as a valuable teaching tool. Working with our hands creates a connection with our mind that nothing else can make. Eliminating touch from our world, tools from our vocabulary, is a loss that limits the mind's ability to synthesize experience. This synthesis is far more important for most young people in school than learning software use. Yet educational districts throw laptops at students like a drug, forgoing their responsibility to educate. They can point at their computer labs and say, "See, we're teaching by training people for jobs."

Computers don't help us to think. They help us to process information. Computer training is no guarantee of a living wage now either. Critical thinking on any level requires taking disparate groups of information and combining them in new forms. Solutions to problems come from this out-of-the-box thinking, not from controlled and programmed thought. This is the advantage that hands-on education has. Students who learn to paint, who can carve wood, or who can dance, whether or not they become an artist, craftsperson, or performer, have acquired experiences that show them how the world is so much alike and yet so varied. It reveals how large the world is, how many ways there are of considering a problem. Hands-on experience teaches students that failure is a part of learning.

It turns out that every job we attempt in the shop is a challenge to our self. Failing this task, bungling that one and murdering the next, we can walk away from work feeling ourselves to be useless. It can be heartbreaking, embarrassing, teeth gnashing. For me it was a frustration to be so unqualified at the bench. In the end, making a choice to work with my hands was as much about managing my sorry self as it was about handling the tools and techniques and materials. I was always the problem, as I kept getting in the way of my success.

We must train ourselves. Not to make spoons or jewelry or paintings or chairs but to be more competent, more forgiving, more patient. If we were simply training for production, there would be only engineering geared to cost-benefit analysis and not the value of Quality. But if you are truly interested in making changes in your work, if you are attempting to do work of Quality, then the work to be done is on you.

Embracing my failure is like holding a new dance partner in my arms, and I must hold her close and breathe her in while we step on each other's toes throughout a song. I must learn to hang onto her for dear life for she is my salvation, the only way through to my education. She can be a challenge to hold on to but I cannot let go. The dance will be worth it.

On a short stopover in Reyjkavik, Iceland, some years ago, I strolled around the small town and headed down a hill toward the bay. I walked past a small, three-story white clapboard building. It wasn't old or particularly attractive. It held apartments inside, as I could see from the small personal items that sat on the window sills. As I was heeding gravity's pull down the hill, I also heard music coming from upstairs. Three instruments, a violin, a flute, and a cello, were playing in a second-floor apartment. They were murdering a piece by Bach, I think. The murder was not in question, I just wasn't sure if it was Bach or Haydn or someone else being killed upstairs. I stopped dead in my tracks to listen to them. They played with such a confident erring. On they stumbled and they never stopped to correct themselves. They pushed forward through their mistakes to the end. I applauded. I had to. I'm not sure they noticed me, but what luck for me to witness their attempt that morning. I looked out at the bay. What fine luck.

Moments like the soloist practicing scales in Portland and the trio murdering Bach in Iceland give me such energy and such hope. These musicians were playing loud for all to hear and tough luck to the world if it was not perfect and the world judged them harshly. There is only one way to the proficiency of the master, and the budding violinist knew it as did the trio. Practice. Keep practicing until the notes have the precision they require. Keep practicing until the work is transformed, until the work transforms you, until study becomes Mastery.

No one anoints you with Mastery. One isn't born with it. You are blessed with talent, but you become a master by repetition. I cannot buy Mastery with a tool, another book, or a week of class or study with a gifted teacher. Those things cannot make you great. Practice does.

As Pirsig quotes in *Zen and the Art of Motorcycle Maintenance*, "Assembly of Japanese bicycle require great peace of mind." He goes on to discuss the importance of this state. The bicycle, the machine, the furniture, has no stake in being right or wrong. No ethical code lives inside a tool. It is the builder that has to bring the good into the work.

It's not about building this stuff. It's an attitude about being at the bench. The task is learning to accept this, learning to be quiet there, learning to slow down. My goal at the bench is to drown out the noise of the world. To forget its insanity, its dangers, its increasing inanities, and strangle, if only for a time, the louder voices inside my head telling me that I can't do this work. If I don't have serenity when I begin to build, I will pull my problems into the piece itself.

At the bench, the problem is always me. It is never the tools but how I handle them. It is not the work that is hard, it is managing my emotions that is the task. Working through the boredom, handling the mistakes, managing my patience, learning from my errors. This is the challenge.

Simplicity is not an end in art, but one arrives at simplicity in spite of oneself, in approaching the real sense of things. Things aren't difficult to make; what is difficult is putting ourselves in the state to make them.
—Constantin Brancusi

PETE FRENCH ROUND BARN

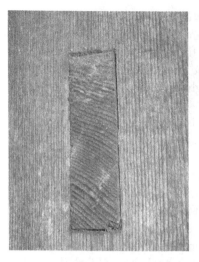

One late summer, I traveled with the beagle to the southeastern edge of Oregon to hike and take in the sights of the Steens Mountains. Close by them in the sagebrush is a structure, a barn hiding in plain sight. Now there is nothing unusual about ranchers building barns. Folks have been ranching out there for a hundred years and more. It's the building itself that's astonishing.

It's a palace. But it is not what you would think of as a palace. It rises up so unexpectedly on the prairie. It's like coming up on Chambord, the hunting chateau in France that looks like Disneyland, in the middle of a huge forest. Yet this barn's placement on the rangeland is so purposeful and baffling. This palace, the Pete French Round Barn, sits all by its lonesome between the mountains and Malheur Lake.

Back in 1883 or '84, Pete French built this 25-foot-tall, 100-foot-diameter barn because he needed a place to run his horses in the snowbound winters of that rugged area. Perhaps Pete had seen a round barn when he was a younger man breaking horses down in California and that gave him the inspiration. He and his crew took months to build several of these on his land.

A giant round roof, shingled with cedar shakes, circles the wooden building. It's held up by juniper poles inside the structure. I walked through the old doorway and I saw that I was on a track. It's a racetrack on the outer ring and inside this is another massive ring of stone. The stones are close to two feet thick and almost nine feet high, with windows to look inside the corral at the horses. It was out of necessity and stubbornness that Pete French built these barns. To run and train his horses for his ranch in any weather. The structure also speaks to a need that was so powerful: to bend the world to his will.

Winters out here are rugged. And yet Mr. French built this amazing structure that looks more like a circus tent than a barn, and it's placed right in the middle of the country where the wind could try and blow it away every winter. Pete didn't care. He had a desire and it would be met. He built three of these round barns. According to history, Mr. French had the iron determination that led him to erect these structures and that also got him killed for his greed to possess all the land that he could own or steal out there. A dispute with an armed neighbor who wanted legal access to traverse Pete's land left him dead.

This is the only barn left standing, and I don't care if you don't like barns or round buildings or horses, the architect or his story. This structure will make you step back and marvel at this man's gumption to create. He had the discipline and a desire that was so powerful that he took the time and considerable effort to build this stone-and-wood corral. It is a work of building art, however crude and simple it may seem, with an elegance and strength that shows through its rough outer skin.

It's an inspiration for me now to remember it and get up and get back to work. I tend to skip the land greed part, but whenever I feel like my life is too hard or I feel like quitting or I'm not getting my share, or I feel like sleeping in or doing everything but what I'm supposed to be doing, if I remember Pete French and those winters, I quit my whining straight away and I get back to work. Mr. French knew that it took effort to get results. No one was going to congratulate him on this. He did the work that he had to do. The effort was part of the reward of doing that work. There are moments of strange inspiration to be found in out-of-the-way places.

20

Letters to Molly

Everyone walks with a limp. Some of us conceal it better than others. It is a fact of our lives that we each struggle with. We have to live with our failings, our inadequacies, believing that we are not good enough, trying to hear it when we are told that we are in fact good, practicing our work through it all.

Here's a story about being an artist. It is a story about being in your head.

I have a friend named Molly who is a jewelry smith, a woman I've known for almost thirty years now who has in the past few years started concentrating all her efforts on her metalwork. She wrote to me once some years ago about how lousy she was feeling about her work. She was lamenting this fact as she rode the bus to her day job doing secretarial work. And in her letter to me, she spoke about her alienation from her fellow passengers, how different she felt being an artist and yet how alone she felt with her own "lousy" work. She asked how could she create art when she felt so repelled from others, so different, and so filled with doubt about her work and its value. I sent her back these quotes sent to me by a student of mine. I wrote:

Molly Dear,
   This is a letter from one of my mastery students. He includes letters from others in it. Take a read.

·

From Paul W. June 17:
   Martha Graham, one of the great dancers of the twentieth century, from a letter to Agnes DeMille, dancer and choreographer:

   There is a vitality, a life force, a quickening that is translated through you into action, and because there is only one of you in all time, this expression is unique. And if you block it, it will never exist through any other medium, and be lost. The world will not have it.

It is not your business to determine how good it is, nor how valuable it is, nor how it compares with other expressions. It is your business to keep it yours clearly and directly, to keep the channel open. You do not even have to believe in yourself or your work. You have to keep open and aware directly to the urges that motivate you. Keep the channel open.

No artist is pleased . . . there is no satisfaction whatever at any time. There is only a queer, divine dissatisfaction; a blessed unrest that keeps us marching and makes us more alive than the others.

Then, from T.S. Eliot, one of the major poets of the twentieth century:

East Coker (1940)
So here I am, in the middle way, having had twenty years—
Twenty years largely wasted, the years [between two wars] of *l'entre deux guerres*—
Trying to learn to use words, and every attempt
Is a wholly new start, and a different kind of failure
Because one has only learnt to get the better of words
For the thing one no longer has to say, or the way in which
One is no longer disposed to say it. And so each venture
Is a new beginning, a raid on the inarticulate
With shabby equipment always deteriorating
In the general mess of imprecision of feeling,
Undisciplined squads of emotion. And what there is to conquer
By strength and submission, has already been discovered
Once or twice, or several times, by men whom one cannot hope
To emulate—but there is no competition—
There is only the fight to recover what has been lost
And found and lost again and again: and now, under conditions
That seem unpropitious. But perhaps neither gain nor loss.
For us, there is only the trying.

•

I wrote back to Paul.

Dear Paul,
There is much truth in these words. Even Martha's last phrase I fear. For just as you once mentioned to me about that iniquitous measure of a mind, an IQ, that it points out the mean, I think that it too often also

142

points out the mean spirited. And so there are those who don't recognize that everyone is taken by this unrest that Ms. Graham mentions.
It is just that some are moved by it. And the rest, the most, squash it
down under the sofa cushions. That's a squished vessel it seems. Forgive
her this trespass against the many, but I fear it true. As for Eliot, this is
marvelous good stuff. Who hasn't felt like he was retreading old ground
again and again? But it is this losing and rediscovery that is our constant.
The striving, the quickening that defines another side of being human.

After the death of my friend Tony a few years ago, I could not find
any reason to create things again. There seemed to be no point. It was
going to end up in rubble as well. More drivel cast up into the wind. But
slowly, and e'en now it's slow, I am finding an urge to start creating again.
There are two measures of hope for me: we have this need to create, to
push against our restlessness, and we can laugh. Through our tears or in
respite from them we can laugh. Thank you much for these gems.
—Gary

•

Then I wrote these words to Molly.

Molly Dear,
Don't we all wish we had written these words. But T.S. Eliot did.
Martha did. And arguably they could be considered great artists. If this
is what assails them, who are we to complain that we too get this crud
in our system? It is a part of the joy and heartbreak of being alone in the
world, alone as artists.

For that's how it works. Creation occurs alone first, overcoming the
doubt and naysayer inside of you and me, the one who says you can't
succeed, you can't do anything but fail. Failure is what you're best at.
Trying to create work. Posh, the only thing you're good at is failing.

Alone is where you are when you have to find that energy to keep
going, to keep seeing what's around that next corner. That curiosity that
you have to keep stoking, even when another side of you is saying that
it's all been done before by much better artists than yourself. When that
side of you is saying what's there to be curious about, what can I bring
to the work that's new?

And we alone, the artists, have this other task as well, to keep the child
alive in us. Keeping the child alive inside, instead of dead like the rest of
the people on your bus. Making that child comfortable and happy and

willing to play, because that's when we do our best work, when we're playing. Not when we're frowning and struggling, down on our luck and on our work, you call this work? It's when we let ourselves run free that we do some cool stuff. Not all of it, but something, something good emerges. As artists we realize that we alone are capable of expressing what's inside of us. We alone are capable of opening those easy doors that we have held shut for so long. Me worst of all! I have held shut these doors for so long. Hiding behind doors of perfection, doors of worry, doors of doubt.

What if we could just do our work, whatever came into our heads without that critic, that constant critic who hates EVERYTHING I do? What if we could do work without that voice always carping on? What if we could pick up that little goblin with the huge voice and put him in a bottle and put a stopper in the bottle and listen to his muffled carping, and get on with our work. How much freer that would be. We can't get rid of the damn carp, we can only put him aside for a while to do the work we were sent here to do. And some of it will be shit, some of it will be trite, some of it will send you to the moon while leaving others speechless with shock over your inability, and some of it will leave you yawning with boredom and disgust while others rave about what an original artist you are.

You can't figure out this stuff. The best you can do is enable yourself, put yourself in the best possible place in order to do your work. And try to keep the voices in a bottle. Of course you need to be critical of your work, your work needs to grow and mature, but you need first to let it grow a little ragged, a little wild now and again, and then you trim it back, then you find the right branch to leave, the right twig to cut off. Every one of us feels this way at some time or another. It's good to hear we're not alone. Because it's lonely out here, it's lonely inside your head.

At an artists' and writers' retreat called the Vermont Studio Center some years ago, I spent some time figuring out my next move as a furniture maker, as a creative person. At the end of two weeks there we had a party and one poet said to me, "It's so good to be around other people like me, because no one understands this life except us." Certainly not the people surrounding you on the bus.

I have another story: this friend of mine traveled all over the world. He would carry his inflatable kayak with him to go exploring whenever he could and wherever he would travel. And travel he did, country to country. He had been to Croatia many times, Prague, he had been an election supervisor in Kosovo. He also traveled the back country, hiking, kayaking. Every day he would wake up and ask himself, "What am I going to do today?" A life rich with possibility was his.

Then in Europe on one of his trips, he was stepping off a train and he slipped, or I don't know, perhaps something more sinister occurred, perhaps he was pushed. In any event, he fell and broke his back and became paralyzed. His legs were gone. He could do some work with his hands and arms. His wheelchair now supported his weight. He said to me last week, "I used to wake up and hit the door and go out and see what the world had to offer me. And now I have to live inside my head."

I was stunned. I said to myself, "I always live inside my head."

Some of us do go out and grab the world. I realized that my friend did it so he wouldn't have to listen to what was inside. Some of us stay inside because we're afraid of what the world will do to us if we go out to grab it. Somewhere in the middle is a spot where we have the guts to go out and touch the world a bit while keeping our thoughts alive inside our head. It's in this middle place that we get a chance to create and to touch others. And most importantly to impact ourselves. Good luck, my dear, with your work. It will come. Just let it.

—Love, G.

•

Molly wrote back.

Thanks Gar,

It's good to see those words (and like the typical aspiring writer I wish I'd written them). I cried for the struggle of it all. I'm off to the studio. I sure hope this acid fades. People kept looking at me on the bus as if I had gangrene.

—Take care, love ya, Moll

•

In truth, the writer's problems are usually psychological, like everyone else's.

—Richard Hugo, *The Triggering Town*

THE ROAD TO MASTERY

I have at my studio a program called the Mastery Study Program. The program lasts full-time at the bench for an intensive nine months or part-time over two years. Students build nine different furniture designs in their own style over this stretch of time. Once a Mastery student asked me when he was going to finally get good at this stuff. When does Mastery come? I wrote Marty back this note:

> Congratulations! You have already done a great deal and you have reached the first wall. You have done a great deal of work and are miles past from where you started but you will come to a wall. This first wall you will scale. When you scale it, you will come to another wall. Scale that and you will find a third. Once that is scaled, you will be on top of the wall on a promontory. From this viewpoint, you will be able to see the next hundred walls you have to cross. They will stretch out into the hills in the distance. Once you scale them, you will marvel at how far you've come from where you began. You should by all means at that third or fourth wall congratulate yourself. You will also see then how far you still have to go. Enjoy the view.

∽

If we knew early on how our choices might affect us, to be able to read the future, to see down the path of our lives, would this knowledge hold us back? It might be too frightening to proceed, to make the decision to work so hard, if we really considered how long these lines we've cast might take to ripple through a lifetime. Would knowing that uncertainty and doubt were going to be my guideposts instead of certitude and a safe future, and that there was some type of reward, however difficult to imagine, wouldn't this be a worthwhile leap to take?

We have no prescience to guide our hand, to help us choose except by our gut and by our intuition, which most of us ignore as faulty anyway. We often feel a hint inside us, a warning sign, but we turn our back on it. We think ourselves into a deadly relationship, or into the worst kind of schooling, or the wrong desk at the wrong office of a dead-end job we devote our life to. We convince ourselves, we work hard at convincing ourselves, Yes this is right. My gut is wrong about it. This is right. I should stay in this place.

Until the day comes when we have to notice that pain in our sides. The one that we have ignored for so long, aware of it but working like a Zen monk to ignore. Like the arm that has gone numb on me as I sleep crookedly on the couch. It is in a terrible and painful position but I'm too lazy to move. It wakes me up and I notice the tingling that seems to say, "Oh, this is going to be uncomfortable to get out of." Most of us do our best to ignore this recognition. We become masters of hiding this truth from ourselves. Like a bubble that blossoms from a leaky water line or a small rip in the fabric that promises to pull apart, that truth will reveal itself. It will come when we can admit that something does not feel right, when we have to say, "No, this is wrong. I have to change it. Something isn't right."

Have no regrets. Follow your instincts. Your choices are only made for you. Only you are living your life so why not defy expectations of how you were raised or what you were trained for?

Vinny, a wise friend of mine, decided to start medical school at the ripe age of 44. He said to me, "Your choices don't have to make sense to someone else, just to you." He was also very smart and tremendously dedicated to the idea that he could not fail himself. He could not pass up the chance to be his best self, different than the plan or expectations already in place for him, only to regret it later on. Ask yourself in a week, a month, or a year if you will look back wishing that you had made that decision. To make the move will be hard, and it will take years of practice for you to become who you are, but it will be right. You must start now. If you just wake up and take whatever life throws at you every day, this won't get you to your goals. Be specific, be ready, be frightened of not trying above all.

Remember the Mark Twain quote, "Twenty years from now you will be more disappointed by the things you didn't do than by the ones you did do. So throw off the bowlines. Sail away from the safe harbor."

Enjoy the journey. Listen to your gut, your heart, follow your instincts. Choose wisely.

⤳

I have come to this bittersweet realization about my choices in life as well. Life doesn't care. No one gets a participation award from life. If I die tomorrow, I will be gone, a few will weep my passing, and then the waters will close over me and my presence will be mostly forgotten by all the others desperately trying to live their own lives. Life doesn't concern itself with whether I live or die. The universe, on the other hand, has a great interest in me while I live. The universe listens.

Therefore, send messages out to it. Ask the universe for help and it will come to you in some fashion. Keep pressing forward. You will have to do your work even if you don't know where it will lead you. Because in truth you will not end up on the shore you set out for. It will be a new, strange, and unforeseen place. Help is guaranteed to come, just not in the way you expect. Not in the neat little tied-up-and-ribboned package you dreamt of, but it will come in some fashion, if you ask.

I have to remember as well that I am in a race. Oh, people will say that I'm not competing against anyone. That's not true. I am competing against time and I will lose. We all lose. In the time that I have, what will I accomplish? Will I give up and say the race is too long or too fast, too hard? Will I tire out early? I am in a race to do my work, the best work I can possibly do. It is important to keep my standards high while others are slacking off saying it's too hard. It's supposed to be hard; otherwise, everyone would do it. It's supposed to make us whine and carp about the pace or the failures we encounter or the simple fact that some days I suck at this work that I have chosen. We all of us feel this way at some time. Then we sleep on it or go for a walk, sit with a friend, or stare out at the mountain. This work is also what makes us feel right. The race is with myself, making myself better each time I go to the bench or the easel or the drawing board. Making sure that I am improving my skills, and staying curious, and getting better at my work each day.

21

Don't Think

Photo by Harold Wood

Don't think. When I am thinking in the shop—about the traffic jams, the stupidity of politicians, the wars—I am not focused. I am not concentrating. I want to be one with the tool and just simply doing my work. I do not want to think about how I am holding the tool, I simply hold it. If I do this well, then time will melt away and the work will come from my hands. This is the place I hope for at the bench. When I know my work, then I never hesitate. There is nothing to think about. There is just the doing.

Lest there be any confusion, when I first get to the bench it still takes time to warm up. To look at it another way, it requires time to shut my brain off and get into the task at hand. If I'm working on something that I have not done in a while, a tool that has laid dormant for months or years and I'm picking it up again, there is a learning curve to travel. With the first stroke, the first part I work on, things feel a bit odd as I'm trying to find how to place myself at the bench. Do I hold this here? Put my feet there? Where do I place the chisel? Learning goes on and with the second stroke, the second part I work on, things feel more fluid, they move easier, the work is smoother. And by the third part, I remember who I am doing this set of moves. I remember it all and the experience comes back to me. But there is always the learning, the remembering that has to be done first. It is simply that the learning curve is much faster for me now than it was at the beginning.

When you watch a master work they make it look simple. One sees a completed piece and you might ask how long it took to make. The answer is always the same. It takes five minutes or fifteen depending on the difficulty of the task, but it took twenty years to learn how. When a master performs a piece, makes a stroke, turns a bowl, it seems to take no time at all for them. The time has already been put into the piece in the years of practice, the years that lend the facility to the master, the years that place that movement into the bones.

↜

Jiro Dreams of Sushi is a marvelous documentary movie made by David Gelb in 2011 that tells the story of Jiro, a sushi master. He owns a humble little shop in a Tokyo subway stop. Ten or twelve stools sit in a patient row at a counter for his customers. It takes months to get a reservation because of the reputation of his food and his artistry. His sushi, the simplicity of his presentation, the flavors he presents are like nothing anyone had ever tasted. His whole life had been spent in this pursuit of becoming better at making sushi. On his vacations, on his days off, he thought only of how to do his work better. How to choose the best fish, how to treat it, salt it, use his vinegars, where and how to best slice it. How to cook rice better, how to prepare it just so. How many minutes to massage the octopus. How to marry flavors and texture and presence. It is his life. He was consumed by becoming better at something that he knew more about than perhaps anyone else in the world. He was eighty-five at the time. He had spent his life learning and was still not done. He still had the curiosity and the drive to want to learn more. What good fortune Jiro had.

In the movie, Jiro's sons and apprentices learn his meticulous approach to every aspect of creating his memorable meals. In repetition was their education and something was practiced daily but only accepted as good when it was done right. One apprentice spent two years practicing to make grilled egg until he finally got it right. He said that he wanted to cry when he finally made it correctly. A food writer remarked on Jiro that he taught his apprentices for free but it would take each of them ten years to be a first-rate chef.

↜

In the late 1990s I was teaching a week-long class at a crafts school in Colorado. My neighbor next to me teaching in the pottery studio was a

Japanese living treasure in ceramics, Takashi Nakasato. He had been honored by Japan for his contributions as an incredible potter and for his lifelong work in the field. His daughter Hanako was his assistant and student at his workshop high in the Rocky Mountains. At that time, I would not have placed the two in the same family. The small man with the mischievous smile and the bent look to him, his worn hands and quiet dignity, and the young woman with her spiked hair and her jewelry-decorated face, an armada of earrings cascading down her eyebrows. But there were father and daughter both working in clay. He was the past, the tradition. She was the hip, the craft as it was to become. He and I were both so busy that we became only nodding acquaintances.

But I had heard of her tasks.

It was her job as his assistant to do many chores for him throughout the days of class and translate his lectures into English. Her work as his apprentice, however, was different and quite simple. Make a pot. It takes minutes to do this when you are skilled at throwing clay. Make a pot. And she would. Make a pot, but then crush it. Make the same pot, the same shape again but crush it. Repeat. And she did this for her hours of practice. Make the same pot with the same shape and learn that shape and learn the movements and learn how to hold her hands and how the clay felt under them and how the water moistened and eased the work and how the speed of the wheel made a difference and how the light changed how the pot looked and when the blue of the sky made your hands move in a certain way and if a bird sounded how this affected the pot, how the pot changed even as it looked the same to others—and with each throw, with each pot, she became more practiced.

She learned this pot and she took it inside herself. She took this knowledge into her hands, her eyes, her bones by practice, by repetition. She trained her hands to feel it, her eyes to see it, her breath to breathe the next pot into life. Each time. Each time the same. Precisely the same and different. She was learning Mastery.

In our world, in this culture, we think of such practice, such discipline as mythic. Sonny Rollins was already a well-known tenor sax player when he took a sabbatical to practice his saxophone on a New York City bridge. Cal Ripken played in over 2,600 baseball games in a row. Nowadays, it's enough to say I've studied 10,000 hours. I'm a master. Or I took a two-day class making [fill in the blank].

Perhaps 10,000 hours is enough. If your field of interest is small.

I gave a luncheon talk to a group of surgeons. I took on the subject of Mastery, and I asked them, "In your education were you a brilliant surgeon mastering your skills after 10,000 hours?" Heads shook vehemently no. "A good surgeon?" Many heads waved no. "A surgeon beginning to learn his or her trade?" Yes, heads agreed. "It's not possible to become truly good in such a short span. It takes years of grateful study. Grateful because if you have chosen well, this is no longer work but your life's work. How fortunate to be able to discover the depths of your field. There is no end in sight. The more you study, the more you will learn how much more there is to learn. That's how it is. You are just beginning your journey."

I know that it took me years to become proficient. And years more to master this work, to have precision. It doesn't happen like a stroll down the block and suddenly you turn a corner. Mastery takes time and one day you will look up and watch or listen or see what you've made and understand that your work has a clarity that it didn't have when you started. It just happened all of a sudden but over many years. An overnight success after a lifetime of work! Enjoy the pace of it. The work only gets better. Plus I will always know that I have the skill in my hands and my heart and no one can take that from me.

> When you are drinking water, drink water, drink only water. That is meditation. You must not drink other things, such as your worries, your plans—wandering around in the realm of your thoughts.
> Thinking prevents us from touching life deeply.
> — Thich Nhat Hanh, *True Love*

ABNER RIDGE

Years later, almost thirty-five years later from my first hike up it, I pulled out my map of Abner Ridge and there was that penciled-in trail on the side of the mountain. I wanted to walk that trail again, this time with the beagle. We had to go past Klickitat Falls, up the ridge, and then find those old pencil marks.

The trailhead was in a different spot from what I remembered but we found the falls fairly soon and they were still beautiful. We headed up the ridge. The Abner Ridge trail had somehow grown longer over the years. It was not just long; it was painful and long. The switchbacks each seemed to take miles. I hiked for hours to get close to the top of this ridge.

Hiking in the forest can be exhilarating, a race against yourself or time, a challenge to surmount. Or it can settle into a slow, steady meditation on the forest, your place in it and in the world. It can be a slow and tedious march. This one was a long trip uphill with only the beagle to talk to. He was older then too, about ten years old, so he stayed in line pretty well. The walk took hours with no views except of trees. At one of the switchbacks I finally got a glimpse out between the trees north, maybe to Washington. Mostly what I saw some distance away were a lot more trees. It was nice to get this new sense of scale but as soon as I turned around it was back up into the forest.

The trail wound along the side of a long slope. A beautiful tall dark grove of conifers took over one section of the walk. We walked between their trunks, then around them to the switchback, and finally I looked through the tops of them down at their bases below me. This was a slow perambulation of a tree's growth habit.

After four hours of hiking, we finally got up to a small spring and pond. There was a bit of grass to rest on. I set down my space blanket and got out some lunch. The beagle was my new best friend then and we shared a bit of a sandwich. I was tired, I had to admit. This trail just didn't want to stop and it was kicking my butt. It kept going on forever. I wanted to turn around. I had seen enough trees for one day. It had been a good hike, but getting home would be good too. We had plenty of daylight but it had been a long day. Why keep pushing if there was nothing to see up here? The map said View, but where was it? I had no clue. Maybe time had muddied the view or my memory of it. I kept thinking about the long walk home. Down hill is tough on the knees.

22

Tools Have Magic

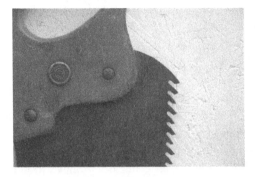 There are machines now, run by computers, that will grab a stack of ¾" sheets of particle board and send them through a saw, spin them, cut them to predetermined sizes so that another machine can rout them for slots, and drill them for holes for hinges and shelve holders. Then a worker assembles these parts to make a cabinet that might last perhaps ten years. These machines are considered tools of industry. They make a cabinet shop money, making boxes for a hungry market.

The tools that lie on my bench are different. They have magic in their grip. These tools that scatter across my shop, that hang in my tool cabinet, that I lay in my drawers and shelves have power. They too can do amazing things, but even sitting dumb and dead on my bench they carry a hint of potential, a promise of mastery. They open up a world of possibility.

What is it about a tool in my hand that makes me feel such a sense of potential? Tools are unlike any other object we touch. Yes, books may give us a feeling of promise and a plate of food a sense of repletion, but a tool or instrument can be admired for its function, the beauty the maker conferred to it, its stolid serenity, its pure dead-on purpose to do one job well. A hammer isn't a saw and never will be, unless in a moment of frustration you've tried to turn it into one. The same can be said for the saw. There is purpose in how I handle them.

That saw I hang on my studio wall is more than a buck saw. It's also a symbol of hard work, of effort, of skill and knowledge. It speaks of a time when the value squeezed out of hard work wasn't done by nut-tightening computer precision. It's a symbol of our need to put our hands on the tools that will help us feel better about ourselves. They can be used for harm as well as good, but a tool from a kit in my hand says something about how I want to face the day.

Grabbing my phone does not yield that same feeling. A phone is a symbol of reliance for most people, not independence. It is a symbol of our willingness to put our head into another screen, get our messages filtered, our world view skewed, and our problems solved by asking Siri. Many people experience the world largely through a screen now. We live in a world that is working to eliminate touch as one of our senses, to minimize the use of our hands to do things except poke at a screen. And designers are working hard to eliminate even that. Read Richard Kearney's fascinating essay in the *New York Times* called "Losing our Touch." The philosophy professor from Boston College writes about how people organize sex now through a screen with online dating services. These users have coined acronyms to message their willingness to have sex, their level of touch. Forget using hands to hold, fingertips to caress, they can only message one's expected level and area of intercourse. The driving engine of the internet has long been pornography, but how far away from each other do we have to get in order to be comfortable? We distance ourselves even in our most basic urges.

We have not simply forgotten how to use tools and make things or fix stuff that is broken. That's sad and lamentable. We have forgotten how to feel the world except translated through our screen. This mediation by others is a loss of personal choice that masquerades as freedom to the masses. It in effect yields our choice to content providers and their own biases and agendas.

Instead with my took kit in hand I can say, "Here's my bag of tools, let me try and fix that."

We make a connection with tools between our mind and our hands. I think this connection is one that is required for us to feel right. I believe that long ago we learned to think by using our hands, not the other way around. Our hands could make movements that gave us advantage and our brains started to develop around these concepts. Tools allow us to consider cause and effect: the lever, the wedge, the hammer. They allowed us to build and to make things in order to survive and later to live better.

Walk down to a shop simply to look at the tools. Their promise is there. The magic that is in their grasp, something old and atavistic, something real with smells from decades ago. There are tools that I have a relationship with. I don't simply hold them. There is knowledge and history in this grip. There is in them some kind of a link to a past when our hands meant as much as our brains, when this act meant more than just a handshake on a deal or a way to hold a keypad, when they were our survival. It is the past, then, that we hold in their grip, something deep and essential to us. People have the need to put their hands on tools and to make things. We need this in order to feel whole.

My belief is that we must touch objects in order to mediate the world. When so much of the world has gone virtual, we need to experience the joy and failure of making an object. We love to build things when so few of our jobs offer a sense of progress or completion. The physical act of making things by hand is by its very nature restorative, contemplative, and centering in a way that computers will never mimic. No matter how good one is at a video game, the act of building actual things carries a benefit with it that is hard to quantify with a numerical score. It serves to touch something inside of us that is, for lack of a better word, primal. Our need to create is what got us here, with all the abundance that now surrounds us. So if some of us retreat a little to our shop and to the small world of our bench, it is done with the kindest of intentions. To make a little peace with ourselves and thereby with the world.

> The physical act of making things by hand is by its very nature restorative, contemplative, and centering in a way that computers will never mimic.

There is value in working with our hands. Isn't there something inside each of us that wants to create something new, something our own? To handle the tools on the bench or at the potter's wheel, or to play the violin or guitar. To handle these tools is to search out what secrets hide within them. They can create things for someone who knows their secrets. Knowledge is strength. Isn't knowledge the greatest tool that we have to carry with us?

The skills one needs to make beautiful things with our hands can seem distant and unreachable. The effort required of your arm and shoulder looks like too much, too long a road to travel, too hard to endure. Yet combining the efforts of hand and eye, using these opposable thumbs of ours, using our hands that are connected to our brain and to our heart in some mysterious fashion is a gift. Why not accept and use it however stumbling our first efforts are? Why not take a chance on discovering the talent we possess?

⌇

Technology now in the shop allows me to do many things very quickly by programming machinery to do the work. I am fairly certain this does less for my well-being than sharpening my plane iron and doing the work by hand, although it is slower to do things that way. It is far more valuable to my life to maintain this connection of my hands with my tools and with my mind.

The satisfaction of smelling the cherry as I cut it, the tang of ash in my nose as it's planed, the true magic of cedar shavings in the air, these are things that a good CNC will not give me. My nose fills with these aromas and my hands feel the heft of the wood. Reading each board as I handle it, feeling its weight, touching a spot on a board to hear it ring hollow. I know what this means. There's a crack there. It's not strong; I have to cut it away. I don't simply cut out paper templates and draw them on the board like it was fabric. This material, this wood, remains alive and responsive. It moves when I cut it and acts differently depending on how I show its face to the world. I need to be close to this material to make these decisions. Putting a cut here, not there, because it will be better. I know how to treat the wood.

⌇

My students ask me if I design on a computer program and I have to say that I don't because when I use a computer I'm using such a different side of my brain that has nothing whatsoever to do with design. Sure, if I'm building cabinets and I want a cut list it would be just fine. But when I'm designing a piece of furniture, I don't want engineering to enter the picture until the aesthetic is in place. Almost half of my students take classes because they want to get away from their computers, so why design work on one? My drawing time is therapeutic. It prepares me for the work ahead. Why would I do this job in an hour when I could spend four hours at it and love what I'm doing the whole time.

The difference between these approaches to drawing and to building comes down to a choice made about how one wants to experience the world. In the classical approach it would be presumed that if you have a choice of tools, you would want the best tool you can find for the job. The computer can cut faster, with less chance of error once set up. It is programmed to succeed for you. This is the Workmanship of Certainty that David Pye writes of in *The Nature and Aesthetics of Design*. The opposite romantic version would have us all start by felling the tree, listening to the wood with each stroke, making all of our tools to fit our hand. There would be little room for art because there would be little time for it. Or perhaps there would be no time for creation because the relationship of tool or material to maker supersedes this in importance.

Neither approach works by itself. One gives us only product, the other only process. To be an artist in the world today requires a blending of the two in order to survive, to succeed in making and selling your work. This has to be done in a way that feeds your soul, not saps it. Pirsig posed this dilemma in *Zen and the Art of Motorcycle Maintenance*. It was his understanding that these two views of the world have to merge in order for anyone to be at peace in the world. Technology is not bad in itself. It is how it is used and the effect it has on the maker, the builder, and the mechanic that's crucial. He understood that the classic mode is primarily theoretic but has its own aesthetic. The romantic mode is primarily aesthetic but also has theory. The two can merge and work together at the bench.

Pirsig's goal was to bring these two points of view together to find the essence of Quality. Preintellectual awareness was how he put it. Understanding something before your mind could name it. It's not just seeing the tool on the bench and your knowledge and experience of what it can do, but seeing it and knowing the feel of it in your hand. One combines these two senses together in a preintellectual awareness in order to understand Pirsig's notion of Quality, his Zen approach to living and being in the world.

One doesn't have to be a Zen monk to understand this feeling. A baseball player knows it just as well when he's in a groove and seeing the ball. It's a sense, a feeling, and all the physicality of his swing combines with the calmness in his mind so that he can produce work, a hit, at a high level. The same is true for a musician who not only knows the notes to play but feels the difference as she bends a note in song. Different sides of our brain have to work together to produce our best, our most inspired work.

I teach the synthesis of both a classical and a romantic view of building, I make functional work that is beautiful. It is not, then, a classical versus romantic struggle but one of having both purpose and intention in a piece. We design work that has a purpose, to be a table or chair. It is designed knowing that this design has an effect on the viewer when she sits at this table to eat meals, to write a letter, or to play music. This is the approach that encompasses both ways of understanding reality and presumes the value of Quality for the maker and for the end user.

If we build things as if our lives depend upon it, then the user might sense this. If we care enough about our work to do the work well, then the user will in some small way see this. There will be no separation between what someone is and what someone does. This is Quality, and our culture's pursuit of capital, of fame, of being heard more loudly in a sea of shouting, misses the importance of it. It is Quality alone that will send us floating away on the ocean of work to be done in our life. On this ocean will we find our struggles, our peace, our failures, our hopes and petty jealousies all appear before us, as real and as fleeting as time itself. It is not a choice for everyone. It was the right decision for me. I took the path that was best for my limited skills and capacities, my limps and my tics, my biases and prejudices, so that I could stand at the bench and try my best to do good work.

> He glanced back at the sledge, a bit of refuse in the vast torment of ice and reddish rock. "It did well," he said. His loyalty extended without disproportion to things, the patient, obstinate, reliable things that we use and get used to, the things we live by. He missed the sledge.
> —Ursula K. Le Guin, *The Left Hand of Darkness*

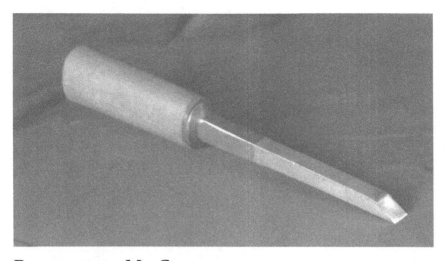

Borrowing My Chisel

This question comes from a former student, Paul F. "If someone asks to borrow a prized chisel, how would you politely decline the request?" My reply: There are several options.

Go Shakespearean:

"What, you egg! Shag-haired villain of treachery!" [And then with a smile] "Begone or I shall have to smite you!"

Or try entreaty:

"Please, please, I invite you. Here are all of my tools, including this my most prized chisel, the one I dote upon, the chisel I grab for when I make only the most important of my cuts. The central chisel at my bench around which my woodworking life revolves. Please gaze upon it and upon them all and marvel at them as do I, but please please do not touch them. Look and marvel."

Finally, be direct:

"When I die, you may touch my tools. If you wish to die today, touch them now."

23

Forgiveness

My first job as a woodworker so long ago was to build a playground structure with Wheaton's help. This project was big for both of us. I had made a choice to try to work with my hands and with wood. I had left behind expectation and security. Wheaton was also figuring out what his next move was going to be. Turns out he needed to be challenging himself with every job he took on.

I was never certain over the years if he ever came to a full sense of peace about the tragedies in his life. Some folks handle a loss by internalizing it, or they meet it head-on and work through it. I think he spent a part of his whole life paying back his old girlfriend Wendy. I also think he was able to forgive himself by working with those bent hands of his. It was a marvel what he could do with them, what he willed them to do, and for what he did for me by showing me the power of forgiveness. It just took a long time for it to sink in to a psyche that believed in my guilt. I realize now that he showed me how I could survive.

Our woodworking is simple, easy stuff by comparison. When I think of what Wheaton had to face, my problems at the bench seem to diminish in size quickly. No one's life changes when we cut a board too short or drop a clamp on a finished project. No one gets hurt when there's tear-out or a drawer is too loose fitting into its home. These things are manageable. Yet the way people feel when they make another mistake in cutting or measuring makes you realize how strong the negative voices are inside us. How loud the critic's voice is.

Jill Bolte Taylor in her book *Stroke of Insight* speaks of her own experience losing cognitive power in the left hemisphere of her brain. Losing those brain functions made her realize what an important role the right hemisphere played for the brain. She also began to understand how the left hemisphere can take over our daily life. The left brain is the storyteller that makes stuff up, that fills in the blanks, that manufactures stories as truth. It's also the worry center, the center of logic, and it's the hemisphere that inhibits our creative side with criticism and judgement.

Everyone makes mistakes. I tell my students that I never worry about offending God by building something too perfect. There are already a dozen mistakes God and I already know about. He can do nothing but chortle at my ineptitude. The difference between the professional and amateur, however, is that the pro quits beating himself up and gets on to fixing things. The whining and crying and arguing with myself usually takes longer than the fix anyhow. This is a lesson that is hard to learn. I have spent days talking my way around a problem, trying to convince myself that it's not so bad, no one will see it. Yet it bothers me every time I think about it. It's far simpler to get to the fix.

Don't get me wrong. It's hard building things and mistakes occur all the time. I have a friend who called her furniture-making shop Flying Hammer Studio. I have been known to throw a tool in the past. I remember kneeling on the floor once, furious over something stupid that I had done. I tried to break my father's mallet hitting it as hard I could against my bench. What my transgression may have been that day escapes me now, of course. I have railed and screamed and acted the complete babbling idiot because I did not, could not, meet my impossible standards, because I could not forgive myself for being human.

Some days are smooth and everything goes right and some days just the opposite occurs. I cut a board too short and then I gouge another with a tool and in my vocal amazement at my stupidity I knock over my half-full coffee cup onto my notes and drawings. Sigh, time to stop, regroup.

Now I grew up with a father who gave me a whole vocabulary of words to use in belittling my stupidity in these situations. Perfectionism was beat into me at an early age and I tried to please this taskmaster. I tried to be perfect, and I couldn't do it. It does not work because I constantly failed. I make mistakes, because—get this now—because I am human. And we humans, we screw up. It's one of our most salient features. We make mistakes, and we can make them over and over again. I try to learn of course. I try to gather information and do better. What I have had to learn over many years was how to manage my disappointment. When I see that I've made a through cut on the wrong end of a board, when I drill through a board instead of stopping short, when I at last notice the scratches of a tool on a piece while I'm putting on a second coat of finish—these can be very disheartening events. It's easy to have noticed them and done it right the first time. The disappointment can be huge. It can fill a room.

In a way it is like pain. Victor Frankl, in *Man's Search for Meaning*, talks about suffering in this way. He writes about his time in a concentration camp watching dead bodies get dragged outside to be disposed of. He survived in a misery so awful I cannot imagine not succumbing to the horror and losing hope. Yet he managed to find within himself the seeds of belief in his and in mankind's goodness. Pain and suffering can fill your world. It doesn't matter the amount of suffering at the time, whether it's starvation or a cramp. Whatever it is, however large, it takes over your universe. As Frankl put it, "If a certain quantity of gas is pumped into an empty chamber, it will fill the chamber completely and evenly, no matter how big the chamber. Thus suffering completely fills the human soul and conscious mind, no matter whether the suffering is great or little. Therefore the 'size' of human suffering is absolutely relative." His suffering was great, far greater than any we will endure at the bench, but he lived through it to write and to help other people. His understanding, his sympathy for anyone's pain, no matter its size, is what inspires.

The same sense of scale, however, is true with a mistake. When it occurs, it fills your world. It is gigantic. It is one more well-lit example of your inability to do anything right. "Is your head even screwed on right?" my father would ask me in disbelief. "What's the matter with you? You couldn't find your ass with both hands." In my early days at the bench, I would let this attitude of my father poison my own mind whenever I screwed up.

꒖

When a problem occurs it takes up all the air in the room. It fills our mind at that moment. It is gigantic. My habit now, rather than smacking myself or launching a tool, is to leave. When a mistake occurs now, I put down my tools and walk outside. I walk down the sidewalk or, if I'm really upset, I walk all the way around the block. I get away from the scene of my error. I get away from the mistake. By the time I return it has shrunk down to its normal size. Then I can look at things and figure out the fix and make it happen. The whining, the moaning, the accusations and recriminations take me away from making the fix, which is usually small and takes far less time than the swearing. Get to it. Next day that mistake is barely a ripple on the pond of memory. And in a few days, forgotten. This method works for me and it was hard to learn but the truth is simple: I am not perfect. It's okay. Do good work. Walk away from the voice that always criticizes. Walk away. Forgive yourself.

Screwing up is a given. Forgiveness is not. Unless you practice it. I have had to learn to manage my disgust with my idiot self that follows me into the shop some days. I am one of the louder woodworkers around, always talking to myself, swearing at my mistakes, huffing and puffing out storm clouds that come and go. But when I practice, when I forgive myself for being human, I can return to the work so much faster. Perfection kills the spirit. It makes me suffer when instead I should be happy for this work. I get to build pieces at a bench with only one knucklehead for a boss. Lighten up, things could be much worse. I could be like so many in this time who one day are told: Your job is gone, clear out by the end of the day. Corporate needed more profits from your division.

Screwing up is a given. Forgiveness is not. Unless you practice it.

⸺

Anne Lamott wrote a wonderful book called *Bird by Bird* about writing and creativity, and about struggling and at times failing at being a writer. This book is on my reading list for my Mastery students because in it she also writes about the critic's voice in each of us. All those critical voices inside our heads screaming at us when we screw up or are about to attempt something new or ambitious. How large they can sound. How difficult they can be to overcome. She talks about having a voice jar to throw all your critics' voices inside of. Let them whine and cajole and chirp at you but put a lid on that jar, listen to these voices for a short time, and then turn down the volume control button on them and get on with your work of getting better. Just throw them in and then close up the jar and turn down the volume. They'll be back when you've done your work. Fear not, they will be back. But for a time, learn how to work without them whispering or shouting in your ear. Make your mistakes and learn from them. As she writes, "Perfectionism is the voice of the oppressor."

The hardest job is to stay focused on what is in front of you. Don't worry about what you can't fix, like your childhood, your mother hating your posture, or your father criticizing your every move. These memories can't be changed; they can't be mended. But they can be ignored so that you can get onto your work. Eventually you'll come to accept the fact that the work isn't usually the problem. Oh you may not know how to do something first time out or maybe you're not sure if something is strong enough. I find that usually these things get done if I just have the courage to try them, and screw them up, and then learn quickly from that experience and move on. The work isn't the problem. I am the problem when I let my voices grow too loud. Do the work. Let it happen. Work on myself.

$\backsim$

A few years back I started to put together a series of free lectures/round table discussions. These DESIGN: Open Houses, as I named them, focused on a variety of topics: Creativity, Inspiration, Design. It was so interesting to hear people's perspectives on these capital-letter ideas.

One night our topic was Curiosity. My guest, Bill, was an accomplished pianist and organist who grew up in a family that valued art and education. They lived in a town in the Midwest that did not. And his point about curiosity was to not squash it. Let your children be curious. Let yourself be curious.

When it was my turn to talk, I chatted about building furniture and the struggles it entailed with yourself, the whole litany of condemnations that follow a furniture maker around the bench. And I was looking at one of my resident students the whole time and it just came to me as I considered his approach and my own about what happens at the bench. I said to him and to the audience that the most important thing I can do in order to build things, the most important quality I need as a furniture maker, is not precision, not planning or determination. The most important thing I need is forgiveness. I have to be able to let myself make mistakes. I want to avoid mistakes, but when they occur, as they will, I have to take it easy on myself. Perfectionism kills and strangles me and prevents me from taking any chances, from being curious, from enjoying what accomplishments I have made at the bench.

Excellence is my standard now. I work to make not my best piece ever each time. I work to make each piece excellent.

$\backsim$

Of all the things that I wish I could have done in this life—forget romance, or my failed enterprises, or the grand dreams that didn't come true—I wish that I could have stood side by side with my grandfather and my father and built something together with them. To have them work with me, without a word, just to have them see me work now. That would have been something.

Since that can never happen except in a dream, all I can do is to make that happen for others now. To show other people how to use their hands in order to create a life for themselves so that they can make themselves and others proud. This life will not be about money or power, except for the power that will lie in their hands. And there is considerable power there, that no one, save time, can take away, and that you can use to create things that have an impact on others. Things of beauty, things that have substance, that grow with life as they grow older. Things that speak to more than one generation for more than one afternoon of froth.

What are the real objects that I can create that will make the world less fractious, less frightening, less filled with the perils of modern life? It is not easy to create work since it is so personal, so revealing. People might laugh at me or mock me. But if I am doing the work that I think is right, then let them laugh. I am in a race but only with myself. I cannot lose this race. I cannot fail or let someone else down. I can only let myself down by not trying.

⌣

The best way is to begin. Make no more excuses about how hard it is, how the timing isn't right, the weather wrong, the effort too much. Begin. Make the choice to begin and good things will come from that. The work will be hard, it can be boring, tiring, depressing, repetitive, not cool, not fast, and not immediately rewarding. It also has the potential to be incredibly satisfying and yield results that are astonishing. One of my very first Mastery study students, Karl, gave me this quote. It's a good one to remember.

> ... Until one is committed there is hesitancy,
> the chance to draw back, always ineffectiveness.
> Concerning all acts of initiative (and creation),
> there is one elementary truth, the ignorance of which
> kills countless ideas and splendid plans:
> that the moment one definitely commits oneself,
> then Providence moves too.

All sorts of things occur to help one
that would never otherwise have occurred.
A whole stream of events issues from the decision,
raising in one's favor all manner of unforeseen incidents
and meetings and material assistance,
which no man could have dreamt would have come his way.
I have learned a deep respect
for one of Goethe's couplets:
"Whatever you can do, or dream you can do, begin it.
Boldness has genius, power, and magic in it."
—W. H. Murray

SHADOWS

I don't want to cut corners. I want to add corners. I want shadows and places to hide. I want light hidden. I want mystery. I don't need the sleek lines of modernism speeding me to some new place. I want spots where my eye stops. Where it can rest. I have had enough of velocity, enough speed for another day of my life. The days go by too quickly now as it is. I want places where I can be quiet. I want what novelist Junichiro Tanizaki says about a Japanese room, that in its dim light it has "the magic of shadows."

This contrasts with our world where everything must be lit up, brightened, so that no one can rest away from the light. It is fine in its way in a shopping mall or office but it is also tiresome. Let there be places where I can sink into shadow and rest there, the darkness seen by candlelight. Does the darkness make the candle burn brighter? Does the space around an object make it stand stronger? The negative space creating the positive. The darkness helping the light. I need to be quiet, I need to be silent with my own desires. In this silence my work, my self grows stronger.

⏤

What if I didn't look for logic or for sense? But looked instead for pattern, or rhythm, or color? I step hard to the left and not to the right. I step on this stone instead of that one. Is there logic in this or is it just the way my foot lands? But oh yes, I change that rhythm with a skip in my step and now I have a new pattern. And on I go, trying to listen for a sound just out of reach.

In this way my stories remind me of how my walks give me something the bench cannot, that my reason cannot. They take me to the bench and to the thoughts that fill my mind as I work. The walking gives me time to roam, my brain the time to go to places unfettered. I let it wander and then bring it back to me and then I see what I can do with this new idea. Walking is a form of meditation for me.

⏤

Statement for Woodworks, a show of furniture at the Contemporary Craft Gallery, 2000, Portland, Oregon:

It must be something in the air there, the predictability of moisture or the gray skies, that seemed to spawn so many woodworkers in the Northwest. Maybe finding a dry shop in the midst of all that humidity was enough to send these makers to their benches surrounded by their wood and tools. But whatever the reason, this region has long seen many of these solitary types muttering to themselves as they carved, built, and turned their beautiful objects in wood.

It is as if, by doing this work, you can capture a moment, freeze it in space, give it form, and offer it life. Of course this takes such an enormous amount of time that you sometimes forget where you started, or the magic changes shape in midflight. But the beauty of delineation, the clarity, the definition of an idea can be such fun. Sometimes it all comes together for you, and it doesn't matter a bit if anyone else gets it, it satisfies something so private, it's all that counts. And at other times your energy, your focus, actually comes through, and it speaks not only to you but to someone else as well.

Then again, it's only furniture. Small strokes or attempts at permanence in a fleeting life. I'm trying to evoke a sense of recognition with my work, maybe an awareness that things worth doing are worth doing well. A life is well spent devoted to this end and that somehow this has a positive effect on others.

꼭

It was many years ago when I still played sports that I become involved through an invitation by a friend to attend Volleyball Church. It was a game that ran once a week on Sunday mornings in a meeting center called Friendly House. We lined up outside the center waiting for Herman and his wife Ruth, who had the keys, to arrive. They would let us in upstairs into the dark wooden gymnasium.

The gym was very old, with windows high up on only two of the walls and screened off to protect them from damage. If one of the big overhead lights was hit by a ball and went out, it was almost too dark to see. The old sodium lamps would take fifteen minutes to recharge and come back on. There was perhaps a foot of sidelines for people to stand on around the court and Herman, with some helpers, would stretch a volleyball net right across the middle of the floor. Before we got to play ball, however, we were invited to sit on the floor and listen to Herman's sermon for that day.

At first, I know I was too pumped to be playing ball to be able to listen to his words. But as he went on, some of what he said sunk through. He often spoke about visualization. He worked with the Olympic team on various training aspects and this was one. Visualize how you wanted to set yourself, where you wanted to launch and jump and hit the ball. It was odd to hear it at the time but it made sense. Imagine where you want yourself to be.

Herman also spoke about forgiveness, because in a sport like volleyball errors are obvious and many, and they affect everyone on the team immediately. It is hard to face your teammates when committing your first or maybe your fifteenth error of the game. It is easier for most competitive people to stamp their feet, throw the ball at the net, swear at themselves, and call themselves or others names. It is very difficult to forgive yourself having done something bad on the court. But he would talk, week after week, in his calm, sure voice about taking care of yourself, taking care of each other. Even in the face of stupidity or errors on the court, of which everyone was capable.

Herman would offer these homilies for us as volleyball players as well as for our lives. To be in the moment only. To learn to forget the past mistake and focus on the present. To be forgiving of others who were doing their best. Part of the egalitarian nature of the Sunday game was its range of abilities. There were players there who could jump to the sky and crush a volleyball. They played alongside those who could barely pass the ball on their best days. They had trouble running the floor and difficulty with the coordination of one foot or hand with the other. Teams were chosen by random count as we stood around on the walls of the gymnasium, and you paired or tripled or quadrupled up as the crowd swelled or waned that week. The first two teams went off onto the court to play. Loser sits. Winner stayed on the floor for three rounds at most and then they too sat.

It's a hard game with only two or three people covering a full court. You have to communicate, you have to be respectful of another's abilities, try to be a good teammate or risk being booed off the floor as a ball hog. We all heard the sermons but we also knew the folks who were easy to play with and those who used up a lot of oxygen in the building. Some of us would move a body or two over before the counting began in order to even teams up or to play with a friend.

In any event, it was a game that had its time in the sun, perhaps for ten years, and then it faded away as did we all. I had occasion some years later to do some work for Herman and Ruth. It was repair work, and I also had to fix a coatrack with some new wooden hooks. These were nothing for me to do, but after that work, every time I saw them they both raved about the beauty of these wooden hooks. One day after running into Herman on the street and listening to him praise me for that simple job, he said he had a story to send me. Here it is.

Cobbler's Story

Hi, Gary! May I give you a story, as promised?

The story is told that if you were a young person in medieval France embarking on a spiritual quest, if you were fortunate you might meet up with someone older, perhaps a teacher, who would say this to you:

"I think I understand what you are seeking. Let me give you the name of someone I know, a cobbler, in Dijon. I think that it might work out well if you were to become his apprentice. If that happens, let me give you one piece of advice. Don't talk with him about spiritual matters; just let him teach you how to make shoes."

So, time passes, and you find yourself in Dijon, and you seek out the cobbler. Sure enough, as it works out, you become his apprentice.

Years pass, and you learn how to make shoes. Year after year, you measure people's feet. You watch them walk. You listen as they tell you about their work, their daily activities, their lives, their yearnings. You make their shoes, you modify their shoes, you repair their shoes. Your shoes tell stories. You make wonderful shoes that enrich people's lives.

More time passes, and one day the cobbler says to you, "You have become a fine cobbler. Your fingers listen to the leather, and your heart listens to the people who will wear your shoes. I am growing old, and soon I will reach the end of my life. I want to leave this shop in your hands."

You begin to protest, but the cobbler goes on. "Now hear me. One day, a young person will come to you, on some kind of spiritual quest. If it works out for this person to become your apprentice, let me give you one piece of advice. Don't talk with him about spiritual matters. Just teach your apprentice how to make shoes."

Warmly, Herman

LETTER TO WHEATON

2/9/2007

Dick,

I wanted to write you about this hike I took. Now it's over a year ago. Sorry for being so slow. I hope you're well. I moved my shop to a building I found close to downtown in southeast Portland. Buried now in work and a huge mortgage. I call it: Living the Dream.

So I needed to go for a hike. Loaded up the truck and me and the beagle and we headed out just for a day to Klickitat Falls. Now I have lots of memories of those falls. You and me snow camping out there. Me taking lots of hikes there, me quitting smoking back in the '80s camping there in Daisy Plain. Lots of memories.

But I had one memory of you and me and Joe Willie, and who knows who, going up Abner Ridge past Klickitat Falls. It was a long series of switchbacks, as I remembered it, up the ridge, and finally we got up so high we couldn't climb up anymore, or at least not with the dog. I remember hitting a wall of rocks that prevented us from going up. I also remember doing some glissading. We had just gotten our new ice axes and so to practice we started jumping down onto this patch of rock-hard ice. I just about broke a rib doing it. Fond memories indeed.

Well anyways, I decided to take the beagle for a walk there. It was a fine fall day. There's a parking lot now there with more broken glass in it than a burned-out Safeway parking lot. Not very appealing. (And may I say that the forest service in their infinite wisdom of paving roads and making parking lots so people in their 4-wheel units don't get muddy have done us all one great disservice. They make access easier, thereby crowding the roads and grinding down the trails but making it easier for knuckleheads to bust into cars.) As I didn't bring anything of value worth stealing, I loaded up without too much worry and off we went.

Klickitat Falls is a beauty. The area is kind of beat-up around it from all the hikers and nature lovers like myself tromping it to death, but it's a gorgeous rock wall of water cascading down it. It's very lovely. It was a nice easy walk up to it, which took us almost an hour.

Now I had a map of this area from years ago when we used it for our hike. And on this map it showed a forest service trail going north around Abner Ridge and heading toward High Pass. But it also showed, marked out in pencil, a route going up Abner Ridge. After three or four major switchbacks, the trail got up to a small lake and then, in pencil, the trail continued on with more switchbacks. It got pretty far up. This was where you and I and Joe Willie had gone up. So me and Jim had gotten to the falls by 11:30. The day was warm. I said to Jimmy, "Let's do it."

We headed up the spine of this old monster for a couple of hours. It was a long hike. Nice tall trees to look at on the way up and then down on while still walking up this trail. I took one little lunch break and then kept trudging uphill. I got one nice view south about two hours up, but that was it for viewing. It was mostly trees. Trees at their base, trees at their top. They start to look pretty much alike after a few hours.

Finally after about three hours of walking straight up, my giddyup had pretty much gotten up and gone. I had counted switchbacks and thought I was close to getting to rocks and timberline, but I just kept seeing more trees ahead of me. I saw some deer checking us out. Fortunately the beagle didn't or I would have been chasing him down still. We finally hit this nice meadow way up high. We moved up the trail past some rock slides and sunshine, past a nice alpine lake, and then we found a stream and some grass. So I followed a little trail across the creek and up the side of a little ridge to see what I could see from there, but it wasn't much. So I headed back to the creek, shucked my pack, and had me another lunch. I figured I had given it a good shot but I was tired. It was getting on toward midafternoon and it didn't look like this mountain was ever going to end. It was whupping me good this day.

But even now, after thirty years of this tromping around in the woods, it gets my goat if I can't reach my goal. I don't fly up the hillsides like I used to just to go fast. The Mazamas taught me and you that day on the Pine Mountain Trail that fast and noisy is no way to travel. But I do like to get a view for all my efforts and there I was pretty

> Keep going, up around the bend. Just go up around the bend and see what's there ... up and up is the only way ...

high up on this ridge and by God I hadn't really seen squat but trees. So I checked the map again. And something in me said just keep going for a little ways more and see what you see. "Keep going, up around the bend. Just go up around the bend and see what's there. We have to be close to seeing something. We have to be." So I argued with myself for a little while and then I gave myself fifteen minutes more of hiking. If we were still in the trees by then, I would turn around. I was tired of going up. But up and up is the only way, I said to myself.

I picked up and moved on. And after climbing for ten or fifteen minutes more I got this glimpse of way down south. Too hazy a day to see much but Mount Jefferson was out there and more beyond it. So I knew I was close. Then we turned a corner on the trail and hit the edge of the ridgeline. We came out on a great meadow lined with flowers and a few spare trees scattered about us, and then there in front of us, bigger than a fist in the eye, was the mountain. All 11,000 and some feet of him just sitting right before me. It was like having a birthday with all my presents and they were all hard to unwrap. And then when I wasn't expecting very much, I got more than my heart's desire. It was a sight. Fine, and my goodness hard not to yell and shout about.

I looked up at the mountain and down I stared at the carved-out river valley some 2000 feet below me that I had walked on sometime before. Distance was mine in every direction. I could look out for miles. This opening, this reveal, stunned me. I had no idea that this was my goal. I

175

never remembered it like this. And truly that trip we took oh so many years ago must have been on a gray day.

Me and the beagle picked our way along this little trail through the remains of the wildflowers and some late bloomers and came up the edge of a precipice which looked down into the Klickitat River Gorge and across to the west side of the mountain. Oh, it was hundreds, thousands of yards away and nothing between it and us but air. And the mountain, well the mountain just kept going up and going up. And if you walked along the edge of the cliffside and looked south you saw the river going south and the canyon it had carved out and the flanks of the mountain looking placid and not steep at all. And beyond were the Cascades stretching out south. It was a fine and stupendous viewpoint and I had almost missed it, and wondered why we hadn't marked it on the map. But it must have been winter or late fall and cloudy.

My goodness, what a view. The beagle and I sat. I took a dozen pictures of my surprise landfall.

By then it was three in the afternoon and we had to get back before we lost the sun. The view was a feast and I could have kept at it for hours. But it was enough to have seen this, to have waited for this, to have put up with the pain for this astonishing picture in my mind. It was time for us to beat it downhill before the sun did.

We hiked downhill and it was an eight-hour hike before it was all said and done. No one had busted into the car. In the parking lot there were four guys on mountain bikes filming themselves jumping off small hill-sides. Not quite as impressive as the mountain view I had received that day, I thought, but there you have it. Folks just have their own interests in life. We made it back okay, and although the beagle didn't seem too impressed by the view I will never forget what getting up off my tired old butt and trudging onward won me that day. It was a gift and I would never have seen it or tried it again if I hadn't gone out on that clear day. Truly I was the lucky man and I wanted to tell you all this. Included some photos. I hope you like them. Anyways I thought about you and that day long ago so I had to send these along.

Your old pal, Gary

P.S. My note that I wrote to myself after getting back home:

Nothing like eight hours of hiking to take your mind off your troubles and put them onto your knees.

I think of that hike up Abner Ridge as bringing something full circle, but it's never that way. The music doesn't swell and the credits run in a life that always stays fulfilled. I keep living, struggling, working through the low times, trying to enjoy the high times. I try to understand my responsibility to pass on to others what I have learned.

All I know is that we, none of us, have much time on this earth. We are each here for a short while. There will be evidence if we choose to do this creative work. We need to make things that leave a mark, a good mark, one that says someone was here trying to do something of value. Speak up, pass along the knowledge that we have so that others may benefit from it and make a life for themselves. Show that the act of forgiveness is one of our most important tasks. Leave good evidence of yourself. Do good work.

Index

ABOUT THE AUTHOR

Photo: Justin Lambert

GARY ROGOWSKI is a furniture maker, designer, teacher, and an author. Since 1974 he has built public and private furniture commissions for clients and galleries nationwide. He was a contributing editor for *Fine Woodworking Magazine* for fourteen years and has written hundreds of articles and several books, including the best-selling *Complete Illustrated Guide to Joinery*. He is also a playwright, novelist, and essayist. Rogowski has taught and lectured throughout the United States and in the United Kingdom, Iceland, and Germany. In 2015, he gave the first-ever lecture in English at the École Boulle in Paris. Rogowski is the founder and director of The Northwest Woodworking Studio, A School for Woodworkers, in Portland, Oregon (www.northwestwoodworking.com). In 2015 he founded a nonprofit organization, Woodworking Ideas Northwest, WIN (www.Winoregon.org), to mentor high school students at the bench.

CPSIA information can be obtained
at www.ICGtesting.com
Printed in the USA
JSHW021243130921
18670JS00002B/219

9 781610 353144